I HoPE You ENJoy THE
BooK + THE Coat!

Jay

Goat

Goat

COOKING AND EATING

JAMES WHETLOR

Photography by Mike Lusmore

quadrille

Publishing Director and Editor: Sarah Lavelle
Designer: Will Webb
Recipe Development and Food Styling: Matt Williamson
Photographer: Mike Lusmore
Additional Food Styling: Stephanie Boote
Copy Editing: Sally Somers
Production Controller: Nikolaus Ginelli
Production Director: Vincent Smith

First published in 2018 by Quadrille,
an imprint of Hardie Grant Publishing

Quadrille
52–54 Southwark Street
London SE1 1UN
quadrille.com

Cataloguing in Publication Data: a catalogue record for this book is available from
the British Library.

ISBN: 978 1 78713 118 7

Printed in China

50 per cent of the royalties from this book will be donated to Farm Africa.

Registered charity no. 326901

Contents

Foreword

There's often a great deal to be sorry about in the world of modern food production. Indeed, there are so many serious problems, worrying issues and shameful practices that it's easy to feel overwhelmed. But there are also innovations, solutions and great ideas – things to be celebrated and enjoyed that offer a fantastic counterpoint to the bad news. These bright, good ideas offer the way forward and it's imperative that we throw a spotlight on them – which is why I'm delighted to be introducing this, James's book.

I first knew James as a talented chef in the River Cottage kitchen. He's now also proved himself a writer and a successful ethical businessman. Cabrito, James's company, was born after he took an uncompromising look at a tough problem within our food system – the wholesale slaughter of the male offspring of dairy goats soon after birth. This euthanising represents an appalling and unnecessary waste. James came up with a canny and viable solution and, by working tirelessly to create a market for those billies as tender young meat animals, has already made a real difference.

As you'll see from his articulate and vigorously argued introduction, James knows an awful lot about goats, about goat dairy products and meat, and about the food industry in general in this country. I'd be lying if I said he and I don't have differing views in some areas – I don't feel quite so sanguine as he does about zero-grazing systems for goats, for instance, and I will always prefer both milk and meat from animals that have lived outside and fed on natural forage for a significant part of their lives. However, I think James and I agree very strongly that we all, as consumers, have a collective responsibility when it comes to the food we eat. We are implicated in the entire story of the ingredients we buy and we have to break out of the what-you-don't-see-can't-hurt-you mentality that is the consequence of industrialised food production.

The good news is that, in some areas at least, we have. Our veal industry, for example, has enjoyed a renaissance as people have woken up to the idea that eating male dairy calves – provided they've been raised in a high-welfare system – is a far saner option than having them slaughtered within hours of their birth.

A comparable sea-change is occurring with goats and James can certainly take much credit for it. In a very short time, he's transformed goat meat from a misunderstood, little-used ingredient to a highly desirable menu must-have. Suddenly, kid has kudos and chefs are flexing their creative muscles to find fantastic new ways to serve it. That's a clear success story.

As our meat and dairy industries continue to grow, we so often lose our sense of what is at the very heart of them – sentient animals. Time and again, welfare and ethics are sacrificed. But they needn't be – and the goat dairy industry, precisely because it is, in its current form, still relatively young and relatively small, can be different. Like the goats themselves, it has the advantage of a certain agility. It can follow its own path.

I believe that people in Britain do care about ethics and sustainability in the food industry. And the more they know about that industry, the more they care. But when there are few alternatives to choose from, how do consumers register dissatisfaction with poor practice? Let's hope that the forward-thinking, positive example of Cabrito – and the fine recipes showcased in this book – inspire yet more creative, delicious and ethical solutions to the problems faced by the food industry. We can certainly all benefit from that. And so can the animals whose meat we eat.

Hugh Fearnley-Whittingstall

Introduction

It wasn't meant to be like this. I was supposed to have a restaurant. I was a young and ambitious chef and the goal, like for most young and ambitious chefs, was to have my own place. Nothing fancy. I'd learned to cook at The Landsdowne in London's Primrose Hill, then The Eagle in Farringdon, and wound up as sous chef at Great Queen Street in Covent Garden, and they are all at the more relaxed end of eating out. Mishmash furniture, no table-cloths… you know the kind of thing. I was going to be one of the many Eagle alumni to take co-founder Michael Belben's idea and put my own mark on it. Luckily (as it turned out) I was a victim of what Robert Burns described as 'the best laid schemes o' mice an' men', and I didn't end up with a restaurant, I ended up with a goat meat business.

That's not to say that my time in those London kitchens was wasted. Far from it. What all these places had in common were great suppliers. Provenance was at the heart of the menus. In the words of David Eyre, the other half of The Eagle's founding partnership: 'Buy the best produce you can and don't f*** with it.' It's great advice for cooks of all abilities, and that experience of the chef–supplier relationship was to come in useful later on.

I have always been interested in the politics of food. I care about where it comes from and how it is grown or reared, so I suppose it was inevitable that I would sooner or later move back home to Devon and work for River Cottage. I spent a few years running the Canteen in Axminster – not far from where I went to school and now live – where the road to a goat business began. A friend of a friend was looking for someone to 'landshare' with. They had an old, overgrown paddock and veg patch that needed looking after but they didn't have the time. My partner Sushi and I jumped at the chance and, like good River Cottage employees, we thought pigs would be perfect for the paddock. The neighbours disagreed. They were trying to sell their house and thought pigs would be smelly and noisy (which they aren't), so what else do you do with a piece of land that needs taming? Goats are the obvious answer.

One of the great things about working at River Cottage is that if you have a question about growing, rearing or cooking you are never far away from someone who knows the answer, so I asked around if anyone knew where I could find some goats. As it turned out, the guy who sold his bread in the Canteen on a Thursday had a market stall in Taunton on a Friday, and next door to him were Will and Caroline Atkinson, goat farmers and cheese makers. Numbers were exchanged and soon we made the trip up to the farm to meet them and the goats.

Will had a problem. He had a load of male goats that he didn't have a use for and he was absolutely adamant that he wouldn't euthanise them, as was standard at the time in the industry. And he saw in a chef from River Cottage

an opportunity to solve this problem. We took four billy goats and put them on the land for the summer; they cleared the paddock of all the scrub and, come late September with their job done, it was time for the pot. We had planned to freeze them and get through them ourselves, but I thought it wouldn't hurt to give one a go on the menu at the Canteen. The first night on the menu the goat outsold the beef. The second night it sold out completely and I had what might prove to be my one good idea. Surely it wasn't just this small Devon town that had an appetite for goat meat? Perhaps, if I could get the carcass right (it was clear a diet of scrub land wasn't going to give the sort of meaty carcasses I would need), then maybe I could help solve Will and Caroline's ongoing problem of the excess billies, and earn a bit of extra cash... Little did I know it was going to take over our lives, empty our bank accounts and be the beginning of a real adventure. Within a year I'd quit cooking and started trying to sell kid goats into London restaurants full time, my dreams of owning a restaurant forgotten in place of a new goal to end the waste of the male kids in the British goat dairy system, which isn't as easy as it sounds (and it doesn't even sound all that easy).

It would have been a great restaurant, though. Wooden floors, open kitchen, hustle and bustle. Maybe one day...

The book you hold in your hands is an attempt to answer all the ethical questions and issues that have arisen since we started selling goats – blissful in our naivety – in 2012. It's also a cookbook with 70 recipes that help answer the question that I've probably been asked the most: 'How do I cook goat?' The Italian Alps may not be the most obvious place to start answering that question, but a little context might help...

Ötzi the Iceman

On 19 September 1991, high in the Ötztal Alps on the Austrian–Italian border, Erika and Helmut Simon were hiking just off a well-worn trail when they came across a body sticking out of the ice. Lying face down, only half the body was visible, the rest being buried in the ice. Thinking it was a mountaineering accident, Erika and Helmut called the police, but it soon became clear that what they had found wasn't some unfortunate, recently deceased climber. The team that came to retrieve the body noticed the strange tattoos on the torso and the unusual collection of objects that clearly didn't belong to a 20th century tourist. The body was handed over to the university of Innsbruck, where it was dated at five and a half thousand years old. He became known as Ötzi. Ötzi the Iceman.

What followed was an international custody dispute, as both Italy and Austria tried to claim Ötzi for themselves. Italy won out in the end as it was decided he was found 100 yards inside Italian territory. It also became a murder mystery, after it was discovered Ötzi had died after taking an arrow in the back.

The value of Ötzi was the unprecedented insight he gave into Chalcolithic, or 'Copper Age', life in Europe at around 3,300 BC. To put into context how old Ötzi is, he was living almost a thousand years before the pyramids at Giza were built, and a century before the invention of the wheel, and he was almost perfectly preserved.

Ötzi's corpse underwent extensive analysis; it is possible that no human in history has been studied more closely. The details the scientists managed to extract about his life are remarkable, and completely revolutionised the understanding of the period. The pollen found in his stomach told them exactly where he had lived. Studying his fingernails told researchers he had been ill a few times in the year before his death, and genetic analysis revealed he was suffering from Lyme disease, the first recorded case in history. However, there are two details that I find exciting and fascinating: he was wearing a pair of leggings made entirely from goatskin – of a design so sophisticated that some historians have speculated that they were the work of a specialist craftsperson – and in his stomach was half a kilo of goat meat.

Ötzi lived at a defining point in European history: the transition between the Stone Age and the Bronze Age, a moment when humans ceased to be hunter-gatherers, moving across the land as nomads, and began to settle into farming. This transition led to the stratification of society and the start of what we would recognise as civilisation – and central to his life were goats. For Ötzi and thousands like him, all across Europe, the goat would provide a vital source of nutrition from its milk and its meat, and long after the animal had been killed it would still be protecting him from the wind and rain.

The case of Ötzi is remarkable in and of itself, but for someone like me, who believes goats have acquired an undeservedly shabby reputation, it's a great example of that injustice. I will try in this book to reshape the image of the goat. Forget the image of Billy Goat Gruff trip-trapping over a bridge. Or the smelly, scrawny, ill-tempered billy tied to a post, living off plastic bags and the clothes of anyone unfortunate enough to get too close. Goats are noble creatures of great utility, and it's time someone put some work into their PR.

Goats weren't prized just by Ötzi and his people; they spread throughout Europe into any habitat that would support them, allowing humans to carve out an existence in many places that would be uninhabitable were it not for the goats they kept. Goats are extraordinary animals that have been at man's right hand for as long as he has used it to pull a plough or bang in a fence post. Today, we have some of the best food you can put in your mouth coming from the milk and the meat of goats; recipes and crafts that have been perfected by societies through the centuries. How and why then did goats become 'the poor man's cow' of history? This seems an extremely unfair label to slap on these versatile, intelligent and hardy animals.

As we can see from the work Farm Africa are doing today in Eastern Africa (see pages 34–7 for more on this), the unique characteristics of goats are helping people, particularly women, to become self-sufficient, manage their environment and become better politically represented. Yes, all that from working with the humble goat.

What do they have to offer in today's world? Few of us have the sort of connection to livestock that Ötzi would have had, so are they still as valuable? What part do they play in the modern farming mix? What are the lives of the goats in the modern system of today and what is the future of goat farming? How does the business my girlfriend and I started five years ago fit into the goat dairy system, and what challenges have we overcome to get where we are today? And, perhaps more importantly, can you still buy Ötzi's goat leather trousers?

The Goat's Place in History

Farming shows up in the archaeological record in the Fertile Crescent – an area of land stretching from Iraq to Egypt – between 10,000 and 12,000 years ago. It is a matter of debate as to how quickly it became widespread or whether it was a result of the amalgamation of lots of different technologies and practices that collectively the literature calls 'Proto-farming'.

Goats were the first livestock animals to be domesticated. There are clear signs of the manipulation of goat herds in the Zagros Mountains in Western Iran around 11,000 BC. What manipulation means in this context is again up for debate. I have found anthropologists are rarely definitive on anything. It could simply mean culling of the herd's weakest animals, or a more involved 'steering' of a herd's movements. The most convincing argument I have read is that the routes to domestication of animals were hunting strategies evolving through time. There is evidence of animals being pursued and herded into enclosed spaces for slaughter. It isn't hard to imagine the small step to the management of captive animals.

The success with goats is thought to have led to the quick domestication of other species. This was a revolutionary process that began the move for humans towards a sedentary lifestyle away from hunter-gatherer. There were clear advantages to farming for these communities, mainly the increased security given by access to a predictable food supply, although it wasn't an easy start. The animals brought diseases with them, and farming, rather than hunting and gathering, meant a much less varied diet. The life expectancy of those early farmers was far lower than that of their nomadic forefathers.

Goats began to spread out of the Fertile Crescent and into Europe, mainly through the Danube valley, and into North Africa, possibly due to climate change making the area drier and pushing the farmers in search of better conditions. By 8,000 BC goats had reached Italy, and a thousand years later had settled in France, turning up in Britain by 6,000 BC. By the time early trading posts were set up by the Persians and the Greeks on the Mediterranean coastline at around 5,000 BC, goats were firmly established in these early societies as central to farming. It's a wonderfully evocative image: the hustle and bustle of those early trading stations, goats being herded on and off boats alongside cargos of spices, wine and barley – but it is also instructive. This is evidence of goats becoming valuable for more than just subsistence living; they were becoming involved in trade and, in some cases, being used as currency.

Why were they considered so valuable? The answer lies in the goat's characteristics. They are remarkably versatile, thriving in environments that are too difficult for other livestock – areas that have greater slopes, less water, rockier soil, places where cattle and sheep simply can't graze well. They aren't aggressive and they reproduce regularly, and it's this that offers a supply of milk to the human farmer. Humans were consuming fermented dairy products like yoghurt and soft cheese long before they drank liquid milk. It seems counterintuitive. Obviously there would have been some experimentation with milk – you don't arrive at cheese without individuals playing around with it – but on a civilisational level, people had little interest in liquid milk.

There are advantages to fermenting milk. Firstly, it makes it more digestible. Lactose intolerance was the norm in early humans (Ötzi was found to be lactose intolerant) and it's only since humans have been farming, with the spread of a genetic mutation, that we have developed an ability to digest lactose. The rapid spread of the lactose-tolerant genetic mutation is an indication of the success these early adopters had. Until relatively recently, in areas of the world without large-scale dairy farming, like South America and East Asia, lactose intolerance levels were still at around 70 per cent in the population.

Fermentation reduced the problems associated with lactose intolerance, but this would not have been the primary reason to do it. Fermentation gave people the ability to store and transport milk. It's a happy coincidence that fermentation breaks down the lactose and makes it more digestible, but its principle function, as far as the early farmers were concerned, was its durability. Durability in the immediate sense, as it pertains to the individual farmer at the time. The areas in which goats thrive, those hills and rocky slopes, would often be far from concentrations of human habitation. Making cheese allowed the storage of a product that, without that transformation, would have a minimal shelf life. It allowed them to bring it back to people and gave them an asset to trade. It also applies in the broader sense, as many of the techniques for fermentation learned thousands of years ago are still in use today.

It might be pushing things a bit far to say that without goats we might still be roaming around the Central Ethiopian plains or painting our thoughts on to the walls of caves in South West France, but across Europe goats have occupied ecological niches that have allowed humans to make a living in almost every environment Europe has to offer. Those communities have endured and today we see the skills learned in cheese making have grown and developed into large-scale manufacturing and been applied to the modern international market.

Spain produces 165,000 tonnes of goat's cheese a year and is responsible for a quarter of all the EU's goat's milk production, most of it from Andalusia. Greece produces around 400,000 tonnes of goat's milk a year, while France, with probably the world's most sophisticated industrialised food production system, produces 655,000 tonnes of goat's milk and 99,216 tonnes of goat's cheese. In the UK we produce 1,820 tonnes of goat's cheese a year – a tiny amount in comparison. Goat dairy production has never been part of the pastoral mix in the UK and that is down to the choices made by farmers in Medieval England.

Archaeological evidence for wool production in the UK dates back to Anglo-Saxon times, but the trade that was to come to dominate the medieval economy really got going around 1200. English wools, especially from the Lincoln breeds, were the most highly prized in Europe. Very little of the raw material was processed in the UK. Wool was valuable and lightweight, so easily transported. The majority was sent to Flanders, in modern-day Belgium, where it was processed by Europe's best weavers. The trade became central to the economy of England, so much so that Edward III went to war with France partly to protect the wool trade (and his own taxation revenue) from the French.

From the late medieval and into the early modern era, the connection between farming, the wool trade and manufacturing became so developed it was the thing that everyone did almost to the point of obsession. If a peasant had a parcel of land and it was suitable for sheep, they put sheep on it. Whereas it might not be economically viable to milk a goat, with sheep you get three products in one: the milk, the meat and the fleece, with the fleece the major value item.

Then came the Enclosure Acts that fenced off large areas of land and gave wealthy landowners the opportunity for scale by allowing the accumulation of large flocks of sheep and cattle. By then the norms of farming in the UK were set, and goats had no part in it. England began producing more cloth, and agricultural workers, after being pushed off their land, took up jobs in urban centres: this was the beginning of the Industrial Revolution.

The unique blend of the UK's ecology and market forces excluded goats from the farming picture and therefore excluded the meat from the dinner plates of the population. It used to take some time for foods to assimilate into culture, as traditional recipes would be passed down through the ages, with slight regional variations. As trade brought new ingredients into cooking, additions would be made. Italian cooking is a great example of this. Pumpkins, tomatoes, gnocchi and pasta are all thought of as central pillars of Italian cuisine. But pumpkins, tomatoes and potatoes are, of course, native to the Americas. Not until after trade routes with the New World were established in the 16th century would any of these things be part of Italian cooking – and they probably pinched pasta from the Chinese, too.

Today, with international travel and global media, food culture and trends can change much more rapidly, and Britain's food culture is unrecognisable from that of 40 years ago. Very little of what we consume on a day-to-day basis is indigenously British, and what the term even means is debatable. The words pork, beef, mutton and veal are all derivations from the French, brought to these islands after the Norman invasion. Now we all love ramen, tagine and salami. We have imported and incorporated food culture from all over the world, but stubbornly not goat. It sticks out like a marrowbone from the crust of a St John pie.

The wool trade can explain why goat was historically never part of British food culture, but why it continues to be viewed with suspicion, given

maud mylk · ꝫ flessh þ[er]wiþ.
caſt þ[er]to pouder galyngale ꝫ
of ᴣᴣ· flo[ur] of rys ꝫ col[our] it
wiþ alkenet · boyle hit · ſalt
hit ꝫ meſſe hit forþ w[ith] ſug[er]
and pouder douce.

Oynons y stewed · xlviij

Tak oynons ꝫ ſtop he w[ith] garlek
y pylled ꝫ w[ith] gode erbes y
hakke ꝫ do he ī an erþen pot
raſt þ[er]to gode broth ꝫ whit
grece · pouder fort · ſaffron · ciantes
ꝫ ſalt ·

Losyns · xlviij

Tak gode broth ꝫ do ī an erþen

the revolution in our eating habits in the past half century, is more difficult to understand.

The Domesday Book shows goats were common in England. In my home town of Axminster in Devon, it records twelve smallholders who have one cob (horse), five cattle and twenty goats. Cows and sheep had a sophisticated food production and by-product industry to feed into. They leave a mark on history and industries whose ancestors survive today. Pantaleone de Confienza wrote about British cheese being sold in Antwerp markets in the 15th century, but as far as we can tell there were no goat's cheeses being made for commercial purposes. Goats aren't referred to in the works of William Shakespeare, Geoffrey Chaucer or the diaries of Samuel Pepys.

Goats were used purely as subsistence animals by the peasantry, and the peasantry were illiterate, so very little in the way of record survives. Goats are the animals of subsistence farmers across Europe, but in that context it is a poor man's animal in a society where almost everyone is poor: the animal of people living on the margins in small-scale farms without the pasture to graze or means to buy cows.

That separation between rich and poor is reflected in the recipe record. In the Middle Ages the only recipe books came out of the royal courts or the houses of the nobility and archbishops. Sadly they are few and far between. The first recipe for goat in the English language, 'A brewet of Almany' (see opposite), appears in *Forme of Cury*, a handwritten manuscript by the Master Cooks of Richard II in 1390; then only nine kid (or *kidd*, or even *kydde*) recipes survive, and four of those are duplicates. These books are circulating around the kitchens of the aristocracy and being updated every few decades, so the duplication is no surprise, but that leaves only five goat recipes across almost 600 years – and they disappear completely after 1650. There is a brief trend for goat in the 19th century as recipes begin to filter back from the Raj in India, and a goat pilaf recipe appears in 1892, but it is very much a peripheral meat.

Animals became more than just a part of pastoral production; they became status symbols. While beef becomes the food of the rich, goat meat remains the food of the poor, and once it is considered the food of the poor it is tainted and the aristocracy won't be seen to be eating it.

Further condemning the status of the goat is that the goat's primary product was the milk; they were never kept solely for meat. The selective breeding and feeding regimes that meat animals have had to improve their confirmation and yield have never been applied to goats. The secondary nature of the meat would again have lessened its perceived value. The carcasses they produce are still seen as inferior to other meat animals.

Evaluating the goat's place in British history has been made harder by the fact that goat bones look a lot like sheep bones. There is almost no contemporary written record of peasant life, so most of what we know of it comes from archaeological digs and, until recently, the assumption has been that it was sheep remains being found. There are far more goats recorded in the Domesday Book than are accounted for in the records. However, DNA technology is helping to build a more accurate picture of homestead life, and I hope there will be a re-evaluation of the role of goats in Medieval England in the coming years.

Goats and Modern Farming

Goat dairies are a tiny part of the farming mix. There is as much milk produced by dairy cows in a single day as there is in the goat system in a year. The two strands are operating in very different markets. However, I think the goat dairies are a great snapshot of the wider farming industry, and offer an insight into the good things the British farming industry is doing, as well as some of the challenges it faces.

There are about 45,000 commercial dairy goats in the UK, producing milk for both drinking and cheese manufacture for a market worth £60 million. Domestic sales have been predicted to grow at anywhere between 10 and 70 per cent. The real growth in the industry, however, is expected to be in export which, as long as the dairies can keep up, could grow by up to 500 per cent. A good news story all round, right? I certainly think so, but why do we hear so little about the successes in modern farming? My explanation is that British farmers are so worried about negative publicity that they hold back in talking loudly about the things they are good at.

If you have livestock on farms you will occasionally have dead animals – old age and sickness are unavoidable – but it is undeniable that a goat's life chances are greatly increased by being in the dairy system. For example, in a commercial dairy herd, mortality rates during kidding are around 3 per cent. Without a farmer's intervention you would expect 15–20 per cent. You can push this argument further: goats in the dairy system are free from cold, wet, hunger and predators, and when they are sick they get treated. They will occasionally feel fear in the same way we do when the doctor comes at us with a needle holding a vaccination, but by and large the animals will live contented lives. The academic description of this situation is 'the symbiosis of domestication' – the idea that in return for the meat or milk the animals provide they get security, and I think it has some merit.

In a strictly Darwinian sense, farmed animals are the winners. They are almost guaranteed to pass on their genes. In broader terms it doesn't make any sense to talk about these animals outside of that symbiosis, and in relation to the condition they would experience in the wild. They simply don't exist outside of our conception and realisation of them as food. Furthermore, our understanding of domesticated animals suffers from 'Disneyfication'. We anthropomorphise them because we don't have any other way of talking about or relating to them, endowing them with emotions they do not have. Which in turn skews our view of how domesticated animals react to their surroundings. This is well demonstrated in the free-range versus housed argument in goat dairies.

In the majority of modern goat dairies, the animals never go outside. Farmers call it 'housed', critics call it 'zero grazed'. When I started out in goat meat I would definitely have fallen into the second camp. I am emotionally a 'free ranger' and still believe that housing pigs, sheep and cows all year round is unnecessary and wrong, but goats are different. It is a mistake to put all domesticated animals into a single group and say what is right for one is right for all of them. No one would do that with cats and dogs. It's the welfare of the goats, not convenience for the farmer, that has made the decision to keep the goats housed. In short, if you have free-range goats you are going to have more vet intervention and medication.

Goats have not evolved for a British climate. They have feet designed for dry, rocky environments, not soft, often wet ground. This makes their feet susceptible to infection if they spend time on muddy ground. Managing the foot health of a few thousand animals is hard enough when they are on dry straw beds (the goats need their toe nails trimming regularly), but if they were outside then infection would become a real problem.

There is also the issue of managing the goat's diet. Sheep and cows are used to having a large proportion of their diet from grass. Goats are not, and have never developed immunity from the parasites that live on grass. Free-range goats may not get sick from grazing but they may suffer a loss of production: there is a difference between a goat being ill and a goat suffering a loss of production, but to fix both you require medical intervention. This creates an added time pressure, leaving less time to focus on other health issues, and that in turn could risk general health standards slipping across the herd. It also leaves the farmer with a decision to make about the economic viability of the animal in the longer term. Is the output of the animal worth the cost of the medical intervention?

Commercial goat dairy herds are built around what is best for the animal. Anyone who knows goats knows that you can't get them to do what you want. I think it's one of their most lovable characteristics, but it has also meant the evolution of modern goat farming has been towards ever better animal welfare, with the system built around what is best for the animals rather than what is convenient for the farmer. It is a misconception to think that you can't have happy, healthy animals that are also high-yielding, profitable animals. The two things are not mutually exclusive. In fact with goats, specifically, if you want to increase your yields it is essential that you have healthy animals.

Perhaps there is no better example of the drive towards greater yields via improved animal health than the work being done in goat genomics. The farming I have seen is full of innovation and the adoption of cutting-edge technology that, I believe, rivals anything in any sector. Genomics isn't about 'Frankenstein foods'. There is a natural ceiling on the amount of milk a goat will produce so it doesn't mean huge goats, with massive udders pumping out ever increasing amounts of milk. It means fitter, stronger, more resilient animals. There can be a difference of as much as 60 per cent in milk yields from the best and worst performing goats in a herd. The aim is to get all the goats up to the level of the top 10 per cent.

Genomics works on exactly the same principles as selective breeding, which has been employed by farmers for centuries. What you are looking to do is pass on the best characteristic from the best animals in your herd. With selective breeding you would take a high-yielding female and mate it with a male who has been known to sire high-yielding females. You would then have to rear the animal, get it in kid and then measure the milk yields of the female to see if it worked. With genomics you'll know the answer as soon as you test the newborn kid. To do it the old way, across a herd of 2,000 goats, is 25 years' work. With genomics, within in a few years you can replace all the low-yielding animals in the herd with high-yielding ones, increasing the efficiency of the farm dramatically. This is happening in the goat dairies now and it's testament to the industry's willingness to innovate.

One of the unintended consequences of the improved health of the national milking herd is that the goats at the end of their economically productive lives will be younger and in better condition than they have been in the past. They will therefore make much better meat carcasses, and that's good news for carnivores everywhere.

Technology is also beginning to be put to work in the feed. We have all heard about how methane from farm animals is a major contributor to greenhouse gases. As funny as farting farm animals are (and they defiantly are), methane is rich in energy. Goats have complex digestive systems built around the rumen, which works by being filled with millions of microfauna – microscopic organisms. They feed on the cellulose that the animal eats and turn that into microbial protein that the goat eventually digests in the small intestine. What researchers are looking at is to affect the genes in the microbes so they produce less methane – a very exciting line of research because it could have a really big impact on the amount of methane the animals produce. Not only is methane a greenhouse gas, but every time an animal belches out methane it's wasting a tremendous amount of energy. The less methane it produces the more of that energy gets converted into food, and the less environmental impact it has.

The thing that links the two examples above – other than that they will make the farms more efficient, make the animals healthier and increase yields – is that they are improvements without an environmental impact. Using genetics and feed technology you are able to increase yields and growth rates without requiring more resource input. There is a recognition in modern farming that it has to move away from old, resource-heavy technologies.

All of the good things happening in goat farming do not insulate it from criticism, however. There are some valid criticisms and one of those led to the creation of our business: how the dairy industry deals with the surplus billy goats. With the exception of a tiny percentage kept for breeding, the male goats – the billies – are not required by the dairies. I think most people understand basic biology and make the connection between needing lactating females to produce milk and the need to get the nannies pregnant for that to happen. The obvious consequence of pregnancy for a nanny is a kid, and nature denotes a 50/50 split between males and females. The females in most cases will either be put back into the herd to be milked, or sold. It is the males that are a problem. You cannot milk a male goat and if there is no market for goat meat, they are euthanised. The dairy industry's justification for this is twofold: they are not economically viable, and it is better from an animal welfare point of view for the goat to be euthanised than to be sold into an uncertain future.

Until recently, the dairy industry's assumption was that the billies were a waste product. And if they are talking about the possibility of 500 per cent growth in the market, that 'billy problem' is only going to become more acute. It's worth focusing on that for a second: a 'waste product', not a 'by-product', and that is an important distinction. A by-product is defined as 'an incidental or secondary product made in the manufacture or synthesis of something else'. A waste product is defined as 'an unusable or unwanted substance of material produced during, or as a result of, a process such as manufacturing'.

These billies were being destroyed and disposed of; 'unusable or unwanted material' if ever there was one. It may seem trivial, this distinction between 'by-product' and 'waste product', but it gets to the heart of the ethical case for me. On a fundamental level I do not think it is right that we allow an animal's life to have absolutely no value, and I don't think we should allow farming practices of this kind. That said, I completely understand why the euthanasia happens. You cannot expect a farmer to rear an animal it has no market for. I have never met anyone in the goat dairy industry who was happy with the euthanising of the billy kids, and as soon as we came along and offered a solution the industry has supported and encouraged it.

The wider point to be made here is that there is a culture that allows the food system to be wasteful, and we are all complicit. Producers and retailers know there are wasteful practices in the farming system but neither side acknowledges it, and they therefore do nothing to combat it. Consumers are complicit because we don't ask enough questions about where food comes from or how it is produced. There is a wilful ignorance on the part of retailers and consumers who – in a race to the bottom on price – accept cheap and convenient food without question. I have found it extraordinary that when I explain the billy problem to people, they nod their head and say, 'Right, yes, of course...' Such is the disconnect that people don't realise male offspring are a consequence of milk production. As consumers we don't scrutinise the food system enough, which allows the sort of unacceptable practice such as euthanising billy goats to happen.

It is incumbent on me to make the nuanced and detailed argument; to explain the reasons and leave it to the consumer to decide whether they are going to support us by buying our product or not. People are smart enough to make their own decisions when given the facts. In the case of the billies, that means explaining that if you are a vegetarian who doesn't eat meat because you don't think animals should be killed to feed humans, but you eat goat's cheese, you are part of the problem rather than part of the solution. As outlined above, eating goat's cheese directly contributes to the euthanising of the billies, so if you eat goat's cheese, or consume any goat dairy products and you want that system to be sustainable, the best thing you can do is buy some goat meat every now and again.

I am an optimist by nature and optimistic about the food system. Changes are possible but it is hard and expensive to retrofit new, more sustainable systems in giant food chains that have been built up over time with a different set of priorities, like being as cheap as possible. In recent years, positive changes have come in the free-range movement; in 2012 free-range eggs outsold caged eggs for the first time. Larger retailers are responding to consumer demand for better traceability and food that is more sustainable, and I believe there are real opportunities for small producers who are more nimble, ethically focused and more skilled than large producers.

Consumers have the power to make changes through the purchasing decisions they make, and this is what I try to help facilitate when talking about the goat dairy system. If you allow consumers to see the consequences of their purchasing decisions, then I think they will make what I believe to be the right choice. That isn't always easy to do. One problem is 'greenwashing' – the practice sometimes employed by companies of spending money and resources on advertising and marketing their green credentials rather than actually designing and implementing polices that minimise environmental impact. Going back to the statistic about eggs, what does 'free-range' mean when it comes to eggs? Probably not what you think; does 64,000 laying hens under one roof in a multi-tiered system sound free-range? Not really, but legislation is chipped away so that this term and others like it begin to lose all meaning. The clouding of the meaning of terms like 'organic' and 'free-range' is of course good news for producers who want to co-opt the 'green' label but who don't want to bear the cost.

Sadly, so much of this conversation comes down to cost. If producers and retailers will only reserve well-reared and ethical products for the most expensive lines, then good produce becomes the preserve of the rich and we have a kind of food apartheid. That's not a society I want to live in, let alone a food system I want to contribute towards. The 2013 horse meat scandal was infuriating and upsetting because it was simply the exploitation of those on lower incomes: the meat didn't turn up in the higher end or luxury brands. I have sat in the meetings and had the phone calls where buyers try to slice more and more off the price, knowing that you want to supply them and they offer scale. Those conversations are disheartening, to say the least. Buyers only care about getting the lowest price, whoever they work for. Think about that next time you stroll down the produce or meat aisle in a supermarket. That stuff isn't on the shelves because it's the best they could get, it's there because it's the cheapest they could find.

Then why am I optimistic? The future of small-scale or artisan production isn't at the mercy of large retailers. The future of artisan production lies in restaurants. Restaurants run by people with a passion for food. Men and women who care about provenance, ethics and quality more than they do about price. These are the source of the trends to which the large retailers feel they must respond, and they will drive the future of British food.

wednesday 8th march

quo vadis

simply shocking 8°c

BITES AHOY!
trout, mayonnaise & lettuce 6.5

baked salsify 5.5

grilled ogleshield sandwich 5.5

smoked eel sandwich 9.5

salt cod, sea kale, spinach & black olive salad 17.5

TODAY'S PIE 19.5

cured trout, shrimp & sea vegetable 'vol au vent' 23

"The QV Aperitivo" 9

crab soup, rouille & croutons 9.5

QV winter salad 16.5

OYSTERS
'morecambe bay' rock oysters 2.5 EACH

beetroot, egg & horseradish salad 8
pork & venison terrine, pickles & co. 8
smoked cod's roe, wild sorrel, salsa verde & almonds 9
octopus, bitter leaves & citrus dressing 10.5
mojama, monk's beard & potato salad 12

grilled ox tongue, beetroot, horseradish & salsa verde 18.5
fried hake, lemon, sage & aioli 22.5
onglet, walnut, horseradish & mustard leaf 22.5
brill, blood orange, tomatoes & fennel 26
rack of kid, celeriac & chard gratin 24

THE SOHO SET

celery & celeriac soup

chicken & guineafowl liver pâté

⋈

wild garlic polenta, ricotta, bitter leaves & hazelnuts

pork belly, fennel, & puntarelle

⋈

pink grapefruit & campari sorbet

walnut & rhubarb mess

19.5 FOR 2
22.5 FOR 3

THE SANDWICH, CHIPS & SALAD 19.5

endive salad 5 ~ jersey royals 6 ~ chips 5 ~ carrots, lemon & dill 6
winter greens 6 ~ green salad 6

PLEASE ASK A MEMBER OF STAFF FOR INFORMATION IF YOU HAVE A FOOD ALLERGY OR INTOLERANCE
26-29 DEAN STREET, SOHO, LONDON W1D 3LL
TELEPHONE 020 7437 9585

Goats on the Menu

I saw a quote from Nathan Outlaw a few years ago in a brief interview for the *Guardian*, and I thought it was probably the most insightful and optimistic thing I had ever read about British food: 'The British restaurant scene is much newer than in France or Spain or Italy, and I don't think we've scratched the surface of what's possible in our own country, with our own ingredients.'

One of the implications of this statement, if it proves to be true and if the British restaurant scene continues to flourish, is that restaurants could be the saviour of artisanal production in the UK, and represent a huge opportunity. It is hard in today's environment to set up a new food business (perhaps any business) without a sustainable element. There is a demand for products that don't negatively affect the environment but which have a story, a narrative that captures the imagination. Today's chefs have grown up in that environment and these influences inform their style. In the time I have been involved in cooking, the chef–producer relationship has completely transformed. When I first started cooking in the early 2000s, the meat supplier was a guy at the end of an answering-machine message. Today, chefs and producers are on first-name terms, and it is a two-way working relationship.

Restaurants have changed a lot too. The economics of opening, especially in London, mean that they are just getting bigger. 150 covers is no longer unusual. Back when restaurants were on average smaller, supplying a product direct to a restaurant would be a useful additional income. Now most of the restaurants I supply are selling more meat than butchers' shops, so it's worth evaluating where the best market is.

Getting our goats onto restaurant menus has lots of advantages that in retrospect look like a clever business plan, but I have to confess we weren't aware of them when we started. In fact the idea that we even had a business plan is laughable. First, you put your product in the hands of some very skilled people and they get the very best out of it. After all, they are chefs and that's what they do. In our case, the goats then ride on the coat-tails of the kudos of the restaurant or chefs. If it's good enough for the world-renowned St John, Yotam Ottolenghi or River Cottage, then it's good enough for anyone. A few thousand people a week will read a restaurant menu. Whether they choose to eat it or not, just seeing our product helps normalise goat as something you can eat and buy in the UK. It is tremendous advertising. That is the biggest challenge that Cabrito has faced: to legitimise goat in the eyes of the consumer. Putting it in some of the best restaurants in the country has helped enormously.

The working relationship between chef and supplier has proved priceless because it offers perspective on our product. We have made changes to our product because the chefs have told us we needed to if it was to work for them. When we first started out, we tried to replicate what I had seen when I was cooking in London: small kids, about 10–12 kilograms. I think we would not have survived as a business had we not listened to the chef – in this case, Tom Harris, co-owner of the excellent Marksman on Hackney Road. On his advice we pushed up the weights of the carcasses to make them cost-efficient and to give the chefs more options. This also meant, of course, that we made more money. That's how important the producer–chef dialogue can be. Thanks, Tom.

The future is challenging for small-scale production. There will always be people who want to do it and they'll find a retail market amongst those willing to pay for a premium product. However, if we continue to rely on the larger retailers the percentage of artisanal producers will get smaller and smaller because the retailers keep driving suppliers to produce everything more cheaply. Restaurants offer a way to create a product without having a large retail buyer perniciously salami-slicing your price every few months. The devaluing effect that slicing has on the product, the industry and the person's labour is vicious.

Chefs don't behave like commercial buyers. Because they work their backsides off for the love of food, there is some understanding of the commitment and drive it takes to be an artisanal food producer. It takes the same qualities to be a decent chef. They aren't disrespectful or just plain greedy enough to ask a producer to be cheaper and cheaper. If they want the product they'll cost it and if they can afford it, they'll buy it. Most artisanal producers don't do what they do because they want to be millionaires. They do it for the love of doing it. They do it because they believe what they produce deserves a place in the food system, and they do it because they care about showcasing the produce that the area they live in can offer. The question is, do we value that? Does society want people who do this sort of thing? Or is just getting enough food to enough people all that matters?

I believe pushing small artisan producers out of business means we all lose. For the good of communities on a small scale and wider society, we need people to do diverse jobs and to produce things. There is value in the diversity of human experience. We can't all work in offices. Small producers making artisan products enhance our lives and can give immense pleasure – not just from the product, but from the process and story behind it.

Artisanal products need to be economically viable on their own terms to survive, and working hand in glove with restaurants is the new model.

The artisanal products seen in restaurants can drive up the quality of the mass-produced stuff, as supermarkets adjust their offering to remain current and reflect new food trends. I'm not saying restaurants are the silver bullet, the answer to all the food system's problems. The food system is vast and this is just one small part of it, but restaurants can be the antidote to the argument that food production needs to be bigger and more industrial because people want cheaper and cheaper food. It is an argument that is self-serving, dished out by people who care more about spreadsheets than good food and the future of food production. There is an obvious need for some food to be produced cheaply, but not *all* food needs to be produced cheaply *all* the time, and no one should be pressured into producing food for less than the cost of production.

The British food renaissance and subsequent explosion of restaurant culture leaves an opportunity for producers to bypass more traditional routes – the walled garden of supermarkets – and go directly to chefs who do care about the provenance and process of food. A customer base that not only gets the best out of their product, but that can help to improve it. From there you can build, and if larger retailers come then they come, but producers needn't be reliant on them. The death of artisanal practice isn't inevitable; artisanal producers just have to adjust to a new market landscape.

Leather

If Cabrito has achieved anything, it has applied a value to the life of a billy goat. Whereas before the animals were euthanised at a few hours' old, considered a waste product, they now have a market value. Cabrito's commitment to ending the waste in the goat dairy system is its founding principle, so it was the next logical step, once we had got the market in the meat going, to find a home for the skins. This proved to be a problem until I met Jack Millington and heard about his plans for the Billy Tannery.

Hides have been tanned for about as long as humans have been hunting animals. By the time Ötzi was trudging around the Alps in his goat leather trousers, the skills had been learned for turning animal hides into everything from shelters to shoes, and a primitive industry in leather manufacturing was already well underway. Ötzi could have tanned his leather in a number of ways: stretching the hides on dry ground and rubbing them with fats and the animal's mashed brain while they dried, or treating them with an infusion of barks, leaves and twigs containing natural tannings and a generous sprinkling of urine. They really were committed to making the most of their resources back then. He also carried a knife that would have been perfect for scraping off the excess meat and hair still attached to the hide.

The Egyptians and Greeks used leather in clothing, and in the kitchen as storage, but it was the Romans who industrialised the process by putting leather to work in the military, and it was the Romans who brought industrial tanning to Britain. Most towns would have had a tannery throughout the Middle Ages, situated by a river that would have provided the power to turn the tanning drums. The introduction of chemicals like lime and sulphuric acid into the tanning process led to the abandonment of traditional methods, as it became a chemical-based process. Demand grew for new types of leather as the Industrial Revolution took hold. Machines required strong belting leathers to drive them, and speciality leathers were made for use in looms. The arrival of the motorcar and the rise in living standards changed leather production again, with the demand for soft, suppler leather for consumer products – meaning tanning became even more chemical-heavy.

At the beginning of the 20th century there were around 4,000 tanneries in the UK. Stricter planning laws and environmental and worker protections applied throughout the 1980s put pressure on the tanning industry in the UK, but it was the market being flooded with cheap imports that all but ended it. Only a few large manufacturers remain and the majority of their raw materials are sourced from overseas, where not only is labour cheap but workers and the environment do not have those protections that Europeans enjoy.

We had tried to find a solution as to what to do with the hides. We had a few tanned. In fact two of the four original goats that started Cabrito are still with us, memorialised in rug form on either side of our bed, but we hit the same problem as the tanning industry and we couldn't get them close to the price of the imported skins. We also didn't have the time or frankly the interest and desire to make it work, and that is what such a project required. We had hit a dead end.

Then Jack Millington got in touch with me. He had the idea of building a micro tannery and trying to restart artisan leather production in the UK – a bold ambition. The first challenge was to negotiate the strict planning and environmental controls – waste management and the pollution of watercourses are the main concerns. Jack worked with Northampton University to devise a non-toxic tanning agent. Such was their success that effluent from Billy Tannery is used as a fertiliser. They then needed the hardware. After transporting the enormous Victorian tanning drums required from an old sheepskin tannery in Yeovil, they had a little trouble squeezing them into a converted stable – but with the help of some straw bales and a tractor, they managed. After four years the Billy Tannery was born on Jack's family farm.

Kid leather isn't just good for those gloves that you are meant to handle delicate people and situations with. It is strong, lightweight and durable, making it ideal for the bags, notebooks and wallets Billy Tannery are making. But it is the soft finish and pronounced grain that make it really beautiful and lend it a luxurious feel.

Having the Billy Tannery take the hides is the last piece of the puzzle for Cabrito. It is another wonderful example of the opportunities out there for artisan production and how the restaurant trade, albeit by a rather circuitous route, is helping make it happen. Being able to step back from the system and see milk, meat and leather is deeply satisfying. It's how things used to be. For centuries, each last resource would be eked out of an animal's carcass. Waste needs to be a 20th century phenomenon. Jack and the Billy Tannery have relearned a skill that Britain had lost, and in doing so have added value to a waste product.

Sadly, Jack is yet to add those Ötzi-style goat leather trousers to the range, but it's early days.

Farm Africa

Right from the start we were determined that Cabrito would have a charitable element. Just as I believe that it's hard to start a food business without an ethical or sustainable element in today's environment, I think it's incumbent on us as a business to take that ethical stance beyond the confines of our product or industry and see where we can help others. If we care about goats, we should care about humans too. The draw towards a charity that works with goats was of course irresistible to us, and so a relationship with Farm Africa was born. 50 per cent of my fee for writing this book, and 50 per cent of the royalties, are being donated to Farm Africa to support the wonderful – and I mean truly wonderful – work they do. So thank you, dear reader, for buying this book and making a small contribution.

Farm Africa has been working in Tigray, Northern Ethiopia for over 20 years, and has worked with over 11,000 women. Most of the households in Tigray are female-headed. The men leave to find casual jobs in the cities and many never return, leaving the women to raise children alone. Women, particularly single mothers and widows, find access to quality livestock hard as

they are traditionally seen as the preserve of male-led households. Being excluded from agriculture, Tigray's main economic activity, means they are overrepresented among those suffering from food insecurity.

The project requires that each recipient of the 'goat package' must pass on three goats to another woman once their herd has grown, turning the recipients of the goats into ambassadors for the system. However, goats require looking after with the same care and attention as they do in the UK dairy system. Farm Africa can't just drop goats into a community and leave them to it. The goal of the project is for the entire system to work when the charity isn't there, so the infrastructure must be built and maintained by people at a local level. Farm Africa has provided training and veterinary support, and has developed a breeding programme to ensure best practice, good animal health and genetic diversity, all with the aim of producing better animals with higher yields in both milk and meat.

Maintaining the project at a local level has meant big changes in the lives of the women involved. It is a community-owned enterprise, run by the community, administered by the community, for the benefit of community – and as the majority of the houses are female-headed they have had to adapt and learn new skills. Farm Africa provides business development training, teaching stock rotation, cash flow and other management skills so they can be sure their enterprises are business-oriented, rather than simple subsistence farming. In the farming system, access to finance is a major issue so the goat projects focus on income generation. Farm Africa is working to establish village savings and loan associations, micro-financing systems that allow the management and growth of the goat communities to be self-sufficient.

The changing roles of women are having an effect on their status in society. Tradition had it that women who spoke in public were 'difficult', but now project participants are more confident about speaking in public and getting involved in community discussions because they recognise that those who do see the benefits. Economically empowering women, giving them access to saving and credit that were previously denied on the basis of their sex, can improve the health and nutrition of the entire family. And the societal changes don't stop there. Women in Oromia report that harmful traditional practices and incidents of violence against women are declining and they are now more aware of their rights, meaning many more women are now claiming their share of property during divorce.

Farm Africa has also made use of the goats to help rehabilitate the local ecosystem. The goat's manure is used to improve the fertility of the land and, coupled with a Farm Africa water management project, the Tigray valley has been revitalised. Locals can now grow maize and vegetables, improving nutrition and feeding the waste to the goats. The project has been so successful in bringing the valley back to life that flowers are now blooming, making it ideal for honey production. This diversification provides resilience should the community suffer a loss of agricultural production. The greening of the Tigray valley has meant households are benefiting from augmenting grazing for their animals, allowing them to increase their herd sizes. Those with fewer livestock have the right to rent out grazing rights to other farmers, another valuable source of income.

In the past the rural poor have had to survive on 'Work for Food' government programmes. Now with the goat project and everything that has been built around it, they are no longer reliant on these emergency measures. The economy of Ethiopia is growing fast, with GDP growth at 10 per cent, and the government has identified agriculture as one of the key areas. Working in partnership with Farm Africa to target government assistance, they are pushing farming from the subsistence to export level, making sure that high-value crops are being grown for that market. It is testament to the usefulness and resilience of goats that they can be used as a catalyst to achieve Farm Africa's development goals at the individual, the local and the district level.

There is an obvious and uncomfortable distinction between the value to the Tigrayian society of these goats and the ease with which we explain away euthanising them in the UK, especially when the usefulness, industry and adaptability of these animals is so starkly illustrated. Once again goats, as they have since the time of Ötzi, have formed a symbiotic relationship with humans and found a niche in which to flourish. I didn't need any convincing as to just how remarkable goats are, but if you did, then this example of how they have helped Farm Africa transform an entire region should bring you round.

Farm Africa's time in the Tigray valley is coming to an end. The model that removes aid dependency and builds resilience against future challenges has the goal of making itself redundant; they will leave behind a sustainable farming system that underpins a local economy, giving the community dignity and hope for the future.

Recipes

If you've picked up this book and thumbed straight to the recipe section then, hello! I can't blame you – it's probably what I would have done, but I urge you to go back and read up because it will help add some context to the recipes ahead. Writing a cookbook based around a single ingredient might seem like a difficult thing to do, but such is the global nature of goat, and so central is it to so many cuisines, that the issue was what to leave out rather than trying to find dishes to put in. I have tried to reflect that global nature, so you will find inspiration from South America to India and from Africa to England, all broken down into cooking techniques: slow, fast, over fire, roast and baked. The conventional wisdom that all goat must be cooked for a long time is thoroughly dismantled: there is a place for those 'low and slow' dishes, of course, but as you will see, there is so much more to it.

The progress we have made in building a market for goat meat has not yet reached the point where the large retailers have decided to jump in. If goat does not yet grace the shelves of your local supermarket, you may have some difficulty in finding the raw materials you need to cook from this book. I would start looking at your local food markets. Increasing numbers of small-scale cheese makers keep a few billies for meat these days, so you may find them selling cuts alongside the cheese – or they might be able to arrange some for you. Your local butcher should be able to source you some; most butchers can get what you want if you ask. Be sure to make the distinction between 'kid goat' and 'nanny goat' when you are getting what you need –

they behave quite differently in the pot! (There is an index on page 208 that tells you which is best for which recipe.) If your butcher can't help, there are plenty of small companies selling goat online, and I would encourage you to find the closest one to you and use them; supporting your local economy is always a good idea. If all that fails (apologies for the shameless self-promotion), we have a lovely website with a shop that couriers nationwide.

Finally, I have some thoughts on cooking itself. Goat may not seem the logical place to start for a novice, or a less confident cook, but it is in fact perfect – precisely because it is central to so many cuisines, it offers the opportunity for exploration. Cooking with goat almost compels you to broaden your cooking repertoire, and I hope that these recipes inspire you to do just that. For absolute beginners, if you think you can't cook, you are wrong – you can. It's just following a set of instructions, a bit like building an IKEA wardrobe, but so much more fun. Don't be afraid to make mistakes, and if you haven't got absolutely every ingredient the recipe calls for, improvise – but please get stuck in.

Interspersed throughout my recipes you will find a few guest recipes. In an effort to sell as many books as possible and therefore raise as much money as possible for Farm Africa, I have recruited some help. I am very grateful to everyone who was kind enough to contribute, and the recipes they have donated are not only wonderful but all very different – again reflecting that global reach and versatility.

Slow

Slow cooking might feel like more familiar territory to those who have tried goat before, or have a bit of experience cooking it. Whenever I am asked what I do for a living and I explain I sell goat meat, more often than not people respond with, 'Ah I love goat curry!' This is both a blessing and a curse. It's great that people have eaten and enjoyed it but we have tried to move the image of the goat on from being meat only good for curry. That said, there are some beautiful curries in the world and it would be impossible to leave them out.

This is perhaps the most international section of the book. Europe, Africa, Asia and South America are all represented and most of the dishes will be familiar, just not with goat. There is a bit of re-appropriation ahead. Most of the recipes would have traditionally been made with goat and only after being anglicized has the goat been removed and replaced by something more accessible. Although you may have made these dishes, they are ripe for revisiting with a renewed authenticity, and they have the added bonus of making your kitchen smell amazing as they cook.

Kid Korma

Because I'm a dairy addict, this and the Rogan Josh (page 46) are two of my favourite curries – the yoghurt (and the almonds in the korma) give such a lovely richness. Neither of these two curries is hot, but you can add a few chilli flakes to the Rogan Josh if you like. I batch-cook a lot at home and these are perfect for that. Double the recipe and freeze what you don't eat, then you'll have homemade ready meals for when you can't be bothered to cook. Serve with rice, naan and chilli and garlic chutney (page 199).

Serves 4

100g/scant ½ cup plain yoghurt
juice of 1 lemon
½ teaspoon ground cinnamon
¼ teaspoon ground cardamom
¼ nutmeg, freshly grated
600g/1lb 5oz diced kid
20g/1½ tablespoons butter
splash of vegetable oil
1 onion, thinly sliced
2 garlic cloves, finely chopped

1 tablespoon grated fresh ginger
big pinch of saffron strands, soaked in
   2 tablespoons warm water
1 teaspoon garam masala
1 tablespoon sugar
40g/scant ½ cup ground almonds
salt
3 tablespoons chopped coriander
   (cilantro), to serve (optional)

In a bowl, mix half the yoghurt and half the lemon juice with the cinnamon, cardamom, nutmeg and ½ teaspoon salt. Add the meat and turn to coat. Set aside to marinate (the longer the better).

Heat the butter with the oil in a large frying pan, add the onion and fry for 10 minutes until soft. Add the garlic and ginger and fry for a few seconds, then add the meat in its marinade, the saffron in its soaking water and half the garam masala, and fry for 5 minutes to thicken.

Add 250ml/1 cup water, the sugar, ground almonds and ½ teaspoon salt, cover and gently simmer for about 1 hour, until tender, giving it a stir every now and then. If the sauce needs to be thicker, cook it uncovered for the last 15 minutes.

Stir in the rest of the yoghurt, a squeeze more lemon juice and the rest of the garam masala, then check the seasoning and serve straight away, topped with coriander (cilantro), if you like.

Aromatic Kid with Aubergine

The aubergines (eggplants) can also be grilled on a barbecue.

Serves 4
for the aubergine
4 aubergines (eggplants)
juice of 1 lemon
30g/2 tablespoons butter
2 tablespoons plain (all-purpose) flour
400ml/generous 1½ cups milk
50g/1¾oz hard goat's cheese, finely
   grated (or use Parmesan or pecorino)
salt and freshly ground black pepper

for the kid stew
1 tablespoon olive oil
800g/1¾lb diced kid
20g/1½ tablespoons butter
1 onion, finely chopped
2 large garlic cloves, finely chopped
1 green (bell) pepper, deseeded
   and finely chopped
1 x 400g/14oz can whole plum
   tomatoes, drained, peeled and
   chopped
1 teaspoon dried oregano
2 bay leaves
1 cinnamon stick
¼ teaspoon Turkish chilli flakes
1 small bunch flatleaf parsley,
   roughly chopped, to serve

Preheat the oven to 220°C/425°F/gas mark 7.

Bake the aubergines (eggplants) for 25 minutes until completely soft (it doesn't matter if the skin burns), then remove from the oven and leave to cool.

While the aubergines are cooking, heat the oil for the stew in a large, heavy flameproof casserole, add the diced meat and fry for 5 minutes until browned all over (you may need to do this batches). Put to one side on a plate.

Add the butter to the same pan and cook the onion, garlic and green (bell) pepper until softened, about 10 minutes. Add the chopped tomatoes, oregano, bay leaves, cinnamon, chilli flakes and 1 teaspoon salt, and cook for 5 minutes to thicken.

Return the meat to the casserole along with 200ml/scant 1 cup water, then cover and cook slowly for 1–1½ hours until the meat is completely tender and the sauce is rich and thick. Check the liquid every now and then to make sure the stew doesn't dry out.

When cooled enough to handle, remove the aubergine skin and roughly mash the flesh, adding the lemon juice. Melt the butter in a pan, stir in the flour and cook for 2 minutes, then whisk in the milk bit by bit, and cook for 10 minutes to a smooth white sauce. Mix the mashed aubergine and the grated cheese into the white sauce and season to taste with salt and pepper.

Check the seasoning of the stew, adding pepper to taste, and salt if required. Serve the stew on top of the aubergine, sprinkled with parsley.

Rogan Josh

Serves 4

600g/1lb 5oz diced kid
75g/⅓ cup plain yoghurt
2 teaspoons chilli powder (add more if
  you want it hotter)
2 teaspoons unsmoked paprika
1 red onion, roughly chopped
1 tablespoon grated fresh ginger
2 garlic cloves, roughly chopped
small bunch of coriander (cilantro),
  leaves and stalks separated

30g/2 tablespoons butter
1 cinnamon stick
5 cardamom pods
1 teaspoon cumin seeds
1 teaspoon coriander seeds
3 whole cloves
3 tomatoes, roughly chopped,
  or ½ x 400g/14oz can tomatoes
salt

Mix together the meat, yoghurt, chilli, paprika and ½ teaspoon salt, and leave to marinate for at least 1 hour, and up to 8 hours in the fridge.

Put the onion, ginger, garlic, ½ teaspoon salt and the coriander (cilantro) stalks in a small food processor and blend to a coarse paste.

Melt the butter in a frying pan, add all the whole spices and fry for 30 seconds. Add the paste and cook for 15 minutes until all the liquid has evaporated and the paste begins to stick to the bottom of the pan.

Add the meat and its marinade with the tomatoes and cook for 5 minutes to break down the tomatoes. Add 200ml/scant 1 cup water then cover and simmer for 1 hour or until the meat is tender and the sauce is rich and thick. Keep an eye on it so it doesn't dry out, adding a little bit of water if it does.

Check the seasoning and serve with the coriander leaves, roughly chopped, on top.

Quick Keema Naan

for the dough
1 teaspoon fast-action dried yeast
300g/generous 1¼ cups plain yoghurt
1 teaspoon caster sugar
250g/generous 1¾ cups plain
  (all-purpose) flour, plus extra for dusting
250g/1¾ cups strong bread flour
1 teaspoon salt
100g/8 tablespoons ghee

for the filling
200g/7oz minced (ground) kid
1 teaspoon garam masala
½ teaspoon chilli powder (optional)
½ teaspoon ground cumin
1 teaspoon grated fresh ginger
1 garlic clove, finely chopped
salt and freshly ground black pepper

Whisk the yeast, yoghurt and sugar together in a small bowl, set aside for 15 minutes until it starts to froth, then tip into an electric mixer with a dough hook attached. Add the flours and salt and knead slowly for 2 minutes, to combine; the dough will be quite dry. Turn up the speed to medium-high and knead for 5 minutes, until the dough is smooth yet firm. Roll into a sausage and cut into 8 pieces. Roll each piece into a ball, put on a large tray, cover with a clean tea towel (dish towel) and set aside to double in size, about 90 minutes.

Mix the minced meat with the spices, ginger and garlic, and season with salt and pepper.

Roll each piece of dough into a circle about 15cm/6in diameter on a floured surface. Divide the spiced mince mixture between 4 of the circles of dough and spread it evenly over. Top each with another circle of dough and re-roll to about 20cm/8in diameter, taking care not to tear the dough.

Dry-fry one at a time in a hot pan until beginning to char in small patches, then flip over and cook in the same way on the other side. Place in a large, wide bowl covered with a clean tea towel while you repeat with the remaining naans.

Braised Kid Shanks with Chickpeas and Chorizo

Years of cheffing in 'gastropubs' means I've cooked thousands of shanks, but always lamb. Kid shanks don't have that uber-fattiness that characterises lamb and so are, in my opinion, superior.

   You can blend some of the chickpeas at the end of cooking to thicken this dish (chickpea cooking liquid makes a great veg stock). Shredded, boiled or sautéed cabbage or kale can be a nice addition. Or you can omit the chorizo and chickpeas from this dish and serve it with a simple side like mashed potato.

Serves 4

for the chickpeas
150g/scant 1 cup dried chickpeas (garbanzo beans), soaked overnight (or use 2 x 400g/14oz cans, drained and rinsed)
1 celery stick, roughly chopped
½ onion, roughly chopped
1 carrot, roughly chopped
2 garlic cloves, peeled and left whole
1 bay leaf

for the shanks
1 tablespoon olive oil
4 kid shanks

3 cooking chorizos, cut into rounds
1 onion, roughly chopped
6 garlic cloves, peeled and left whole
1 carrot, roughly chopped
3 celery sticks, roughly chopped
2 tomatoes, roughly chopped
100ml/scant ½ cup dry white wine
1 bay leaf
250ml/1 cup chicken or kid stock (or water is fine)
salt and freshly ground black pepper
small bunch of flatleaf parsley, roughly chopped, to serve (optional)

Drain the soaked chickpeas (garbanzo beans), if using dried. Place in a saucepan and cover with 3 times the volume of water. Add the celery, onion, carrot, garlic and bay and bring to the boil. Skim off any scum and simmer for about 1–1½ hours or until completely tender, then drain.

Heat the oil in a heavy, flameproof casserole, season the shanks and brown on all sides, then remove to a plate. Add the chorizo to the casserole and cook for 5 minutes until the oil runs out and the rounds begin to crisp up. Remove a quarter of the chorizo and set aside.

Add the onion, garlic, carrot and celery to the casserole and cook until softened and fragrant, about 15 minutes.

Add the tomatoes and cook for 5 minutes to thicken, then add the wine and bay leaf and stir to deglaze and reduce by half.

Place the shanks back on top of the vegetable mixture, pour the stock over the top and bring to a light simmer. Turn the heat to low, cover and braise for about 1½ hours, or until the shanks are completely tender and pulling away from the bone.

Stir in the drained cooked chickpeas and warm through, then add salt and pepper to taste. Remove from the heat and leave to rest, covered, for at least 10 minutes. Reheat the reserved chorizo and spoon over the top with the parsley, if using, to serve.

Kid Mole

This can be made into a mole sauce that you can serve with barbecued, grilled or leftover kid. Replace the stock with a bit of water, omit the kid and cook until just thickened. I've left the dark chocolate optional but if you've got it, use it. The richness and slight bitter tang it lends are worth the effort. If you like you can serve it as part of a Mexican feast with griddled tortillas, red onion, lime wedges and seasoned sour cream.

Serves 4

3 dried ancho or pasilla chillies, stemmed and deseeded
4 garlic cloves, unpeeled
3 tomatoes, halved
4 tablespoons rendered kid fat, lard or vegetable oil
1 onion, chopped
1 teaspoon dried thyme
1 teaspoon dried oregano
¼ teaspoon ground cloves
½ teaspoon ground cinnamon
1 teaspoon ground cumin
½ teaspoon freshly ground black pepper

50g/1¾oz whole almonds
30g/1oz sesame seeds, lightly toasted
1 tablespoon red wine vinegar
50g/1¾oz raisins
600g/1lb 5oz diced kid
300ml/1¼ cups kid or chicken stock (or use water)
30g/1oz dark chocolate (optional)
salt
handful of coriander (cilantro), roughly chopped, to serve (optional)
1 red chilli, finely sliced, to serve (optional)

Dry-fry the chillies in a frying pan over a medium heat for 30 seconds until lightly browned. Transfer to a bowl and cover with boiling water.

Add the garlic and the tomatoes, skin side down, to the same pan and char for 5 minutes. Peel the skin off the garlic and tomato halves.

Heat 2 tablespoons of the fat or oil in a large pan or pot, add the onion and fry for about 5 minutes until softened.

Drain the chillies and put into a small food processor with the charred tomato and garlic, 1 teaspoon salt, herbs, spices, almonds, half the sesame seeds, the vinegar and the raisins. Blend to a paste.

Push the onion to the side of the pan, add the remaining fat or oil and fry the diced meat in batches until just coloured all over, removing each browned batch to a plate as it is done.

Add the spice paste to the pan and fry for 5 minutes, stirring almost constantly until thickened. Return the meat and any juices to the pan, then add the stock. Bring to a simmer and give it a good stir, then cover, reduce the heat to low and cook for about 1½ hours until the meat is tender and the sauce is rich and thick.

Stir through the chocolate, if using, and check the seasoning. Scatter over the remaining sesame seeds, and some coriander (cilantro) and red chilli, if liked.

Kid Osso Buco

I just love osso buco: the bone with a hole. This is another dish I wanted to put in the book because of my cheffing days. Traditionally a veal dish, it was and is one of my favourite things to cook. The classic accompaniment is saffron risotto (as pictured, opposite), but it's great with polenta or roast potatoes too.

Use whole shanks if you can't get them cut across the bone in traditional osso buco style. Or use leg or shoulder steaks. It is best if you can cook the meat in a single layer.

Serves 4

4 pieces of kid osso buco
  (or 4 small whole shanks)
3 tablespoons plain (all-purpose) flour
2 tablespoons olive oil
30g/2 tablespoons butter
2 onions, finely chopped
5 celery sticks, finely chopped
2 carrots, peeled and finely chopped
4 garlic cloves, roughly chopped
2 tablespoons tomato paste
3 bay leaves
1 sprig of rosemary or sage
500ml/2 cups dry wine (white, red
  or a mix of both)

500ml/2 cups kid stock (or use water
  or chicken stock)
1 lemon
salt and freshly ground black pepper

for the gremolata
finely grated zest from the osso buco
  lemon (after pared strip removed)
1 garlic clove, very finely chopped
3 tablespoons finely chopped
  flatleaf parsley

Season the osso buco pieces and dust with the flour, then fry in the olive oil in a large pan until browned all over. Transfer to a plate.

Add the butter to the pan followed by the onions, celery and carrots, and cook gently until very soft, aromatic and starting to stick to the pan, about 15 minutes. Add the garlic and cook for 1 minute. Add the tomato paste and herbs and cook for 1 minute, then add the wine, turn up the heat and cook for 5 minutes until the wine has reduced by half.

Add the osso buco pieces back in and pour in the stock, making sure that the meat is covered (or at least mostly covered) in liquid. Using a vegetable peeler, pare off a strip of lemon zest (saving the rest to grate for the gremolata) and add to the pan. Cover and cook gently for about 1½ hours until completely tender. Taste and adjust the seasoning if necessary.

Meanwhile, mix together the gremolata ingredients. Serve the osso buco in the sauce, sprinkled with the gremolata.

Kid Shank, Apricot and Pistachio Tagine

There was always going to be a tagine in this book. Adding the sweetness of dried fruit to the depth and richness of kid meat creates a dish that is one of the greats of world food. I always have a jar of ras al hanout in the kitchen – it's a really useful seasoning. You can also use 800g/1¾lb diced kid here in place of the shanks. Serve with harissa (page 199) and couscous.

Serves 4

4 kid shanks
2 tomatoes, roughly chopped
2 onions, finely chopped
3 garlic cloves, finely chopped
60g/¼ cup butter, melted
1 teaspoon cumin seeds, toasted
   and ground
2 teaspoons ras al hanout spice blend
½ teaspoon ground turmeric
400ml/generous 1½ cups stock or water
10 saffron strands, soaked in warm water
   for 10 minutes

small bunch of coriander (cilantro), leaves
   chopped, stalks reserved
150g/5oz dried apricots, roughly chopped
1 medium preserved lemon, rind only
   (discard the pulp), roughly chopped
50g/1¾oz pistachios, roughly chopped
honey, to taste
salt and freshly ground black pepper
small bunch of mint, leaves picked,
   to serve

Mix together the shanks, tomatoes, onions, garlic, melted butter, spices (apart from the saffron), 1 teaspoon salt and ½ teaspoon pepper. Cover and refrigerate for a few hours or overnight.

When ready to cook, put the marinated meat in a large saucepan and cook, uncovered, over a moderate heat for 20 minutes until a sauce has formed and thickened.

Add the stock or water, along with the saffron and its soaking water, the

coriander (cilantro) stalks, dried apricots and the preserved lemon, then cover and simmer gently over a low heat for about 2 hours or until the meat is completely tender. Top with a little water if it dries out.

When the shanks are cooked, remove any excess fat from the sauce and add the pistachios, then the honey with salt and pepper to taste. Serve scattered with the coriander and mint leaves.

Kid Khoresht with Rhubarb

This is really good made in a slow cooker, if you have one. Serve with chopped salad and yoghurt sauce (page 201). It can also be topped with rose petals.

Serves 4

700g/1lb 9oz diced kid
2 tablespoons vegetable or olive oil
 (or use butter)
2 large onions, finely diced
½ teaspoon ground turmeric
½ teaspoon ground cinnamon
pinch of saffron strands (optional)
¼ nutmeg, freshly grated

1 tablespoon honey
3½ tablespoons pomegranate
 molasses
500ml/2 cups kid stock (or use water
 or chicken stock)
2 sticks of rhubarb, roughly chopped
salt and freshly ground black pepper

Season the meat with salt and pepper.

Heat 1 tablespoon of the oil in a pan and add the diced meat. Fry until just coloured on all sides, then transfer to a plate. Add the rest of the oil and the onions to the same pan and cook until soft, about 10 minutes.

Add the spices and cook for 1 minute, then add back the meat, with the honey and pomegranate molasses.

Add the stock to the pan and bring to a gentle simmer, then cover and cook for about 1½ hours over a low heat, stirring every now and then until the meat is completely tender and the sauce is thick (cook uncovered after 45 minutes if the sauce is too thin). Add the rhubarb for the final 15 minutes. Check the seasoning, adding more salt, pepper or honey to taste before serving.

West African Peanut Curry

This needs a bit of looking after while it's cooking as the peanuts can catch – the occasional stir and making sure the heat is nice and low beneath it will be fine.

Serve with plain boiled rice, chopped banana or avocado, hot sauce (page 198), chopped boiled eggs, peanuts, chopped (bell) peppers and coriander (cilantro).

Serves 4

600g/1lb 5oz diced goat
4 tablespoons vegetable or red palm oil
1 large onion, finely diced
2 tablespoons grated fresh ginger
3 garlic cloves, finely chopped
2 teaspoons dried chilli flakes or cayenne, or use a fresh Scotch bonnet chilli if you like it hot!
1 teaspoon ground turmeric
1 teaspoon coriander seeds, toasted and ground

1 teaspoon cumin seeds, toasted and ground
1 x 400g/14oz can chopped tomatoes
100g/scant ½ cup peanut butter
100g/3½oz roasted peanuts, coarsely chopped
400ml/generous 1½ cups goat stock (or use chicken stock or water)
salt and freshly ground black pepper

Season the diced meat with salt and pepper.

Heat 2 tablespoons of the oil in a saucepan, add the diced meat and fry until just coloured all over, then transfer to a plate.

Add the remaining 2 tablespoons of oil to the pan, then add the onion and fry until soft, about 10 minutes. Add the ginger, garlic and spices and cook for 1 minute, then add the tomatoes and cook for 5 minutes to thicken.

Return the meat to the pan, along with the peanut butter and peanuts, and add the stock. Bring to the boil, reduce the heat to low and cook, covered, for about 1½ hours, or until the meat is tender.

Remove from the heat and check the seasoning, adding more salt, chilli and pepper where necessary, then serve.

Kid Rendang

It is best to use blocks of tamarind pulp, even though these require a little extra work. Cut off the portion you need, cover with an equal amount of boiling water and allow to sit for 15 minutes until softened. Use your fingers to mash it a little, then push it through a fine-meshed strainer. Use the pulp and discard the fibres and seeds.

Serve with rice and chilli or hot sauce (page 198).

Serves 4

2 tablespoons grated fresh ginger
3 small shallots or 1 small red onion, roughly chopped
4 garlic cloves, peeled
2 fresh red chillies (or more to taste), stems removed
3 tablespoons vegetable oil
2 lemongrass stalks, cut in half
8 kaffir lime leaves
1 teaspoon ground turmeric
1 teaspoon ground cumin
1 cinnamon stick

2 star anise
2 cardamom pods
600g/1lb 5oz diced kid
400ml/generous 1½ cups coconut milk
2 tablespoons tamarind pulp (see recipe introduction)
1 teaspoon palm sugar (or use white sugar)
salt
2 tablespoons toasted coconut flakes or shavings, to serve (optional)

Put the ginger, shallots, garlic and chillies in a small food processor and blend to a smooth paste.

Fry the paste in the oil for 5 minutes until it starts to stick, then add the lemongrass, kaffir lime leaves and all the spices and fry for 30 seconds. Add 100ml/scant ½ cup water and gently simmer until the mixture is completely dry and starts to stick again.

Add the meat and cook for 10 minutes, stirring frequently. Add the coconut milk, tamarind and sugar, with salt to taste.

Cook, uncovered, over a very low heat for about 1½ hours, until dark brown and quite dry and the meat is tender, adding a splash of water if it dries out too much, and stirring well every now and then.

Check for seasoning, adding more salt, tamarind pulp or sugar to taste. Serve sprinkled with the toasted coconut, if using.

Kid with Almonds

This is based on the Elisabeth Luard recipe in the modern classic *European Peasant Cookery* – one of the few cookbooks to feature kid recipes. It really teases out the subtle flavour of the kid.

Serve with crusty bread and a green salad.

Serves 4–6

1kg/2lb 3oz kid shoulder steaks,
  or chopped big chunks on the bone
4 tablespoons olive oil
1 whole head of garlic, cloves separated
  but left unpeeled
2 bay leaves

3 tablespoons chopped parsley
150ml/²⁄₃ cup white wine
200ml/scant 1 cup chicken or vegetable
  stock (or use water)
200g/7oz whole unblanched almonds
salt and freshly ground black pepper

Season the meat with salt and pepper and fry in 3 tablespoons of the olive oil for about 5 minutes, until nicely browned all over (you might need to do this in batches).

Return all the browned meat to the pan, add the garlic, bay leaves and half the parsley and fry for about 5 minutes. Add the white wine and cook for 5 minutes or until the wine has reduced by half.

Add the stock or water and bring to the boil. Turn down the heat, cover and leave to simmer very gently for about 1½ hours, until the meat is completely tender, adding a splash of water every now and then if it is drying out.

Meanwhile, fry the almonds in the remaining 1 tablespoon olive oil for about 3 minutes until just starting to colour. Pound or blend the almonds to a paste using a little of the cooking juices from the pan.

When the meat is tender, add the almond paste, check the seasoning and cook gently for 5 minutes to thicken the sauce.

Allow to rest, covered, for 10 minutes before serving, with the remaining parsley sprinkled over.

Curry Goat

This is perhaps the most obvious recipe to include in the book. I did consider not putting it in – after all, we have spent five years telling people there is more to goat than curry, but like an ageing rock band, we gotta play the hits.

Curry goat can be served with plain white rice, or the more traditional rice and peas, as well as hot sauce (page 198). Take care when handling the Scotch bonnets.

Serves 4

juice of ½ lemon
700g/1lb 9oz diced goat or kid
3 garlic cloves, finely chopped
1–2 Scotch bonnet chillies (depending on
   how hot you want it), finely chopped
2 tablespoons Jamaican curry powder,
   or more to taste
2 teaspoons chopped fresh thyme
   (or use 1 teaspoon dried)
½ bunch spring onions (scallions),
   thinly sliced

1 teaspoon ground ginger
3 tablespoons vegetable oil
1 teaspoon brown sugar
1 onion, sliced
2 teaspoons tomato paste
2–3 medium potatoes, peeled and
   cut into chunks
salt and freshly ground black pepper

Squeeze the lemon juice over the diced meat, mix well and leave for around 5 minutes.

Add the garlic, chilli, 1 tablespoon of the curry powder, the thyme, spring onions (scallions), ground ginger, half the oil and ½ teaspoon each of salt and pepper. Mix well. Cover and marinate in the fridge for at least 2 hours and ideally overnight.

Remove the meat from the fridge and let it rest at room temperature for at least 30 minutes before cooking.

Heat the remaining oil and the sugar in a pot over a high heat then add the onion and fry for 5 minutes until softened. Add the tomato paste and the rest of the curry powder and cook for 2 minutes.

Add the meat to the pot and give it a good stir. Turn the heat down to medium and cook for about 20 minutes, stirring occasionally to prevent the meat sticking.

Add about 250ml/1 cup water, cover and simmer for 1–2 hours or until tender (this might depend on the age of the meat). Add a bit more water now and then if it dries out (you need enough volume to cook the potatoes later).

When the meat is tender, adjust the seasoning, adding more salt, pepper or curry powder to taste, then add the potatoes and cook until tender, about 30 minutes. If you want really thick curry goat, let the potatoes cook even more, so they break down.

Cabrito al Disco

This recipe was given to me by Martin Anderson, aka The Travelling Gaucho. He once shoved a bowl of this into my hand while I was delivering to Temper, the restaurant where he works. It's not just in the book because it has such a brilliant name – it's here because it tastes like it's made by someone who loves you.

New potatoes, peeled and cut into bite-sized chunks, added to the sauce after the canned tomatoes, are a great addition (see photo, opposite). And please, please, please make the humita below to serve with the disco – it's the best side dish in the book!

Serves 6–8

1.5kg/3¼lb kid meat, cut into about
    4cm/1½in cubes
60ml/¼ cup extra virgin olive oil
1 white onion, diced
1 red (bell) pepper, deseeded and diced
2 garlic cloves, chopped
4 tomatoes, quartered
1 teaspoon smoked paprika

1 teaspoon black pepper
2 teaspoons salt
1 teaspoon dried oregano
1 fresh chilli, finely chopped
1 glass of white wine
1 x 400g/14oz can chopped tomatoes
2 spring onions (scallions), finely sliced,
    to serve

Brown the cubed meat in the olive oil, then add the onion, (bell) pepper, garlic and fresh tomatoes and cook until the onions are translucent, about 10 minutes.

Add the spices, salt, oregano, chilli and wine and, once the alcohol has evaporated, add the canned tomatoes. Cover and cook until the meat is tender, about 1 hour, adding a little water if it starts to dry out.

Serve with humita (below) and the spring onions (scallions) sprinkled over.

Humita

½ red onion, finely diced
2 tablespoons extra virgin olive oil
1 red (bell) pepper, deseeded and
    finely diced
1 jalapeño chilli, finely diced

4 ears of sweetcorn, blackened on the
    barbecue and grated
1 burrata or mozzarella ball, chopped
    (save the liquid)
salt and freshly ground black pepper

Cook the onion in the oil until translucent, about 5 minutes, then add the red (bell) pepper and chilli and cook for 5 minutes. Add the grated sweetcorn and cook until tender, about 5 minutes.

Stir in the cheese until melted, adding some of the liquid if necessary. Season to taste and serve with the Cabrito al Disco.

Heart Goulash

Serve with boiled potatoes, rice or pasta. The heart can be replaced with thinly sliced kid meat.

Serves 4

4 kid hearts
3 tablespoons sunflower oil, kid dripping or lard
2 slices smoked bacon, finely chopped (optional)
2 (bell) peppers, deseeded and thinly sliced
2 onions, thinly sliced
2 garlic cloves, thinly sliced

2 tablespoons sweet paprika (Hungarian if possible)
2 teaspoons hot paprika
200ml/scant 1 cup tomato passata
50g/scant ¼ cup sour cream, plus a bit extra to serve
salt and freshly ground black pepper

Cut the hearts in half lengthways and cut out anything that isn't muscle, such as the tubes and ventricles (although the thin layer on the outside of the heart is fine). Wipe off any excess blood then cut into thin slices.

Heat half the oil or lard in a pan, add the bacon, if using, and fry for a couple of minutes to release the fat. Add the (bell) peppers and onions and cook for about 15 minutes until completely softened. Stir in the garlic and paprikas and cook for a couple of minutes, then add the passata and cook for 5 minutes.

Meanwhile, season the heart with salt and heat the remaining oil or lard in a frying pan. Add the heart slices to the hot pan and fry over a high heat until lightly coloured (you might need to do this in batches). Transfer the heart and any juices from the pan to the onion and pepper mix, and stir well. Cook for 5 minutes to combine.

Add about 150ml/²/₃ cup water and 1 teaspoon each of salt and pepper. Bring to a very gentle simmer, cover and cook over the lowest possible heat for about 1½–2 hours, until the meat is very tender and the sauce is rich and thick. Check occasionally, adding a little water if it is drying out.

Once the meat is tender, stir in the sour cream, check the seasoning and serve.

Ivan Day

A German Brewet

I wanted to include this for the sake of historical interest. I was privileged to spend a few hours with Ivan at his Cumbrian farmhouse, talking about food and cooking sausages in a clockwork spit in front of an open fire. His knowledge of food is surpassed only by his generosity with it. He found the following recipe in one of the oldest cookbooks in the English language, *The Forme of Cury*.

> *Take kid and cut them in small morsels or in pieces. Parboil them with the same broth* [referring to a previous recipe], *make an almond milk and cook the meat in it, add powder of galingale and of ginger with rice flour and colour it with alkanes, boil it, season it with salt and serve it forth with sugar and powder douce.*

'Powder douce' was a spice mixture, probably made with a mixture of cinnamon, mace and nutmeg, often ground together with a little sugar. 'Alkanes' is a saffron-like spice that leeches a bright red colour when warmed in oil or water. Sugar – just a little – was used as a seasoning and flavour enhancer for meat dishes during this period.

Romy Gill

Goat Keema

Romy is one of the hardest-working people I know. Her restaurant, Romy's Kitchen in Thornbury, just outside Bristol, turns out some of the best Indian food I've ever had, and she has been a great advocate for Cabrito since we started. This keema recipe is a little beauty.

Serves 4

2 tablespoons sunflower oil
1 teaspoon cumin seeds
1 teaspoon nigella seeds
1 tablespoon grated fresh ginger
3 garlic cloves, chopped
3 red onions, finely diced
3 green chillies, chopped
2 teaspoons tomato paste
1 teaspoon ground turmeric

2 teaspoons garam masala
1 teaspoon tamarind paste
4 teaspoons dried fenugreek leaves
150g/5oz frozen peas
500g/1lb 2oz minced (ground) kid
salt
handful of coriander (cilantro), finely
   shredded, to serve (optional)
1 red chilli, finely sliced, to serve (optional)

Heat the oil in a pan, add the cumin and nigella seeds and fry until they start to sizzle. Add the ginger and garlic and cook for 1 minute, then add the onions and cook for 6–7 minutes.

Add the chillies, tomato paste and 2 tablespoons water and cook for another minute, then add the turmeric, garam masala, tamarind paste, fenugreek, peas and salt to taste, and cook for another 2 minutes.

Add the minced meat to the paste and cook over a high heat, stirring continuously until the fat starts coming out of the goat mince, about 2–3 minutes. Cover and cook over a low heat, for a further 10–15 minutes, stirring occasionally.

Check the seasoning and scatter over the coriander (cilantro) and chillies, if using, before serving with plain boiled rice.

Kricket

Kid Goat Raan

Kricket started life as a pop-up in a shipping container in Brixton, and was such as success that it has grown into a modern Indian restaurant in London's Soho. This is probably one of my favourite dishes in the book. Anything with a litre of double (heavy) cream in it is OK by me. The recipe looks … unconventional, but stick at it. It comes together beautifully in the end.

Serves 10

1 tablespoon grated fresh ginger
1 tablespoon grated garlic
2 tablespoons vegetable oil
1 leg of kid
3 tablespoons Kashmiri chilli powder
2 tablespoons salt
3 star anise
2 cinnamon sticks
6 whole cloves
8 black peppercorns

2 black cardamom pods
4 green cardamom pods
600ml/2½ cups malt vinegar
1 litre/4 cups double (heavy) cream
pinch of saffron strands, soaked in a little
  warm water
2 tablespoons garam masala
chopped mint leaves and pomegranate
  seeds, to serve

In a small food processor or blender, blitz the ginger and garlic together with the oil to form a smooth paste. Rub the leg all over with the paste, the chilli powder and salt, and leave to marinate overnight in the fridge.

Preheat the oven to 200°C/400°F/gas mark 6. Place the leg in a large casserole or pot that has a lid, add the whole spices, vinegar and enough water to just cover the meat. Cover and cook in the oven for 30 minutes, then reduce the heat to 170°C/325°F/gas mark 3 and cook for a further 4–5 hours, until the meat is falling off the bone.

Remove the casserole from the oven, take the leg out of the braising liquid and set aside until cool enough to handle. Transfer the braising liquid to a pan and

boil over a high heat until thickened and the salt levels taste correct. Strain into a clean pan, reduce the heat and add the cream, saffron and its soaking liquid, and the garam masala. Simmer for a further 5 minutes, check the seasoning and set aside to cool.

Meanwhile, pull away the meat from the bone and set aside.

When you are ready to serve, heat a frying pan over a high heat and sear off the meat in small batches to give it a nice crispy exterior. Return it all to the frying pan, add the braising sauce and stir through the goat until it is nicely coated.

Serve the raan sprinkled with chopped mint and pomegranate.

Neil Rankin

Goat Tacos

I was sitting in a reclining chair in the South of France in 2013, flicking through Twitter, when I saw Neil making these tacos at Meatopia, and it changed the way I thought about our product for good: it made me believe that kid could move out of its niche and break into the mainstream. Now at Temper, Neil has transformed the way people think about cooking with live fire, and we have pulled along in his wake. Thanks, Neil.

Makes 10

1 whole shoulder of kid, about
   1.5–2kg/3¼–4½lb
150g/1½ cups masa harina
1 tablespoon olive oil
50g/1¾oz chipotle in adobo, blended
   until smooth
100g/scant ½ cup sour cream
1 avocado, diced
juice of 2 limes
2 jalapeño chillies, finely sliced
1 red onion, finely sliced

small bunch of coriander (cilantro),
   leaves only
salt

For the green sauce
25g/1oz coriander (cilantro),
   leaves and stalks
6 garlic cloves, chopped
grated zest of 1 lime
50ml/1¾fl oz lime juice

Preheat the oven to 130°C/250°F/gas mark 1.

Season the shoulder with salt, place in a roasting pan, cover with foil and cook in the oven for 5 hours.

While the meat is roasting, make the taco dough. Mix the masa harina with a pinch of salt, then add the olive oil and about 100ml/scant ½ cup of water to achieve a smooth dough. If it's too sticky, add more flour; too dry, more water. Roll into a ball, cover in cling film (plastic wrap) and refrigerate until needed.

Mix the blended chipotle with the sour cream and set aside.

Meanwhile, make the green sauce. Place all the ingredients in a blender or small food processor and whiz until smooth.

Once the meat is cooked and tender, remove from the oven and set aside at room temperature to cool, then pull off chunks of meat and use the fat left in the tray to keep it moist.

Heat a non-stick or cast-iron pan on the hob until nice and hot. Roll the taco dough into about 10 small balls, then roll each ball between 2 pieces of greaseproof paper, pressing down to make a flat circle. Dry-fry in batches in the hot pan for 1 minute on each side, and repeat until the dough is used up, stacking up the cooked tacos on a plate as you go.

Build the taco with the pulled meat and diced avocado. Drench in freshly squeezed lime juice, top with the chipotle-sour cream, green sauce, and slices of jalapeño and red onion. Finish with the coriander (cilantro) leaves.

Quick Cooks

This section of the book has lots of recipes that you will recognize: sausages, meatballs, burgers – the sort of easy-to-make food we all eat, all the time. When we started thinking about goat versions of these sorts of dishes I knew they had to have an authenticity. I saw no point in trying to make a goat version of a pork and apple sausage, for instance, as the pork version would always be superior. Instead, we followed the goat to its source and found inspiration there... except, perhaps, for the burgers, but I'm sure you will forgive me for that.

   This is a group of recipes where I urge you to get your hands dirty. When mixing the spices into the sausages or meatballs, get your hands into the bowl and pound and squash the meat with your fingers. Work the meat like you are making bread dough. This will do a few things: it will make sure the spices and flavourings are evenly distributed through the mixture; it will help the texture by causing the proteins to bind; and it will make you feel like you own it, like you've actually made it – and that is a lovely feeling.

   There is some obvious crossover between quick cooking and barbecuing, and plenty of these recipes will cook fantastically well and even be enhanced over coals, so please experiment!

SAUSAGES

Sausages are great fun to make but it does take a bit of time to get everything together, so I make the most of it and make a few different flavours and fill the freezer with them. The mixes can also be enclosed in caul fat as with the Sheftalia on page 100.

Merguez

You can make these with minced (ground) kid if you prefer but, as with this method, keeping everything as cold as possible is important.

Makes about 2.2kg/5lb
(35–40 sausages)

4 garlic cloves, crushed

2 tablespoons salt

1 tablespoon hot paprika
  (not smoked)

2 teaspoons ground black pepper

2 teaspoons ground cumin

2 teaspoons ground coriander

2kg/4½lb boneless kid shoulder,
  cut into strips 8cm/3in long

50ml/3½ tablespoons red wine vinegar,
  chilled

70g/2¼oz harissa (page 199)

about 4m/13ft sheep casings

Combine the garlic, salt and spices, rub into the meat and refrigerate for 15 minutes. Mix in the vinegar, harissa and 50ml/3½ tablespoons of water and put the mixture in the freezer until very firm, about 30 minutes. Chill the mixer bowl and meat mincer parts in the freezer too.

Set up the mincer with the coarse plate and mince the chilled meat, adding any remaining liquid from the bowl to the minced meat. Put the minced mixture back in the freezer to keep it as close to 0°C/32°F as possible. Then use clean hands or the paddle of a mixer to beat the meat for about 50 seconds, until a sticky mass forms; be careful not to let the meat get too warm.

Form a small sausage ball to test for seasoning, and put the rest of the mixture in the fridge. Fry the ball, then taste and adjust the seasonings if necessary, and keep the mixture chilled for up to 3 hours.

Soak the casings in warm water for 30 minutes then drain. Working over the sink, gently run warm water through each casing, looking for any spots that leak – cut out those portions. Place the sausage stuffing equipment in the freezer for 15 minutes.

Set up the sausage stuffer and add the meat mixture. Slip all but 6cm/2¼in of the casing onto the tube, leaving the trailing end untied. Start cranking the sausage stuffer very slowly until the meat emerges from the tube. Now tie a knot at the trailing end of the casing. Slowly crank the sausage mix into the casing, using your free hand to regulate how tightly the sausage is packed; make sure you don't overstuff the casing. When the casing is nearly stuffed, tie off the end.

Starting at one end, pinch off the first link by pinching your fingers around the sausage to separate the filling about 15cm/6in along. Then roll the link toward you 3 to 5 times, creating a twist in the casing. Move down 15cm/6in to form the next link, rolling 3 to 5 times in the opposite direction (this prevents unravelling). If the casing splits, remove the stuffing near the split and tie the casing closed before proceeding. Repeat with the remaining casings and sausage.

Hang the sausages on wooden or metal racks over 2 roasting pans, making sure not to crowd them so that air can circulate around them. Let the sausages hang to dry for 1–2 hours, then wrap in butcher's paper and refrigerate overnight before cooking or freezing.

Orange and Leek Loukaniko Greek Sausage

**Makes about 2.5kg/5½lb
(35–40 sausages)**

2 tablespoons salt
2kg/4½lb boneless kid shoulder, cubed
4 leeks (white part only), trimmed and finely chopped
2 tablespoons extra virgin olive oil
6 garlic cloves, crushed
finely grated zest of 1 large orange

2 teaspoons ground coriander, toasted
2 teaspoons freshly ground black pepper
1 tablespoon dried oregano (preferably Greek)
1 teaspoon dried thyme
75ml/5 tablespoons red wine, chilled
3 tablespoons red wine vinegar, chilled
about 4m/13ft sheep casings

Rub the salt into the meat and refrigerate for 15 minutes, then freeze until very firm, about 45 minutes. Chill the bowl of your stand mixer and the paddle attachment, and the meat mincer parts too.

Fry the leeks in the olive oil for 10 minutes until soft, spread out on a plate to cool then place in the freezer to chill until very cold.

Set up the mincer with the coarse plate and mince the meat, adding any liquid left in the bowl to the minced meat. Add the chilled leeks to the meat and mix to distribute them evenly. Chill for another 10 minutes, then add the garlic, orange zest, coriander, black pepper, oregano and thyme. Using the chilled paddle attachment and stand mixer bowl, mix at a low speed for 1 minute. Add the red wine and vinegar and mix until the liquid

is incorporated and the mixture is uniform and sticky, about 1 minute longer.

Form a small sausage ball to test for seasoning, and put the rest of the mixture in the fridge. Fry the ball, then taste and adjust the seasonings if necessary, and keep the mixture chilled for up to 3 hours.

Follow the instructions for filling the casings, shaping and hanging the sausages as for the Merguez on page 81.

If you would like to smoke the Loukaniko, use a smoking wood such as oak. Set the cooking grate in place and the sausages away from the fire. Cover, positioning the air vent over the sausages. Smoke until the wood and charcoal are burnt out, 1–2 hours.

Two Kid Sausage Pasta Sauces

Both of these are also good served with polenta.

Serves 4
For the sausage mixture base
1 small onion, finely chopped
2 tablespoons olive oil
6 kid sausages (pages 81–2), or use
    minced/ground kid), skinned and
    roughly chopped

2 garlic cloves, finely chopped
½ teaspoon dried chilli flakes,
    or to taste (optional)
salt and freshly ground black pepper

Fry the onion in the olive oil until soft, about 5 minutes. Add the sausage and cook until just browned, then add the garlic, chilli flakes and salt and pepper to taste and cook for 1 minute.

Tomato, Chilli & Nutmeg

1 quantity sausage mixture base (above)
1 x 400g/14oz can whole plum tomatoes,
    drained and chopped
50ml/3½ tablespoons double
    (heavy) cream
¼ nutmeg, freshly grated
400g/14oz dried penne pasta
    (or other pasta tubes)
freshly grated Parmesan, to serve

Cook the sausage mixture as outlined above, then stir in the tomatoes. Lower the heat and cook for about 10 minutes until the sauce is thickened and rich. Add the cream and nutmeg and check the seasoning.

Meanwhile, cook the pasta until al dente, according to the packet instructions, then drain, reserving some of the cooking water. Stir the pasta through the sauce, adding a little cooking water if you need to let the sauce down, and serve topped with freshly grated Parmesan.

Broccoli and Rosemary

1 quantity sausage mixture base (above)
small sprig of rosemary, leaves finely
    chopped
300g/10½oz dried orechiette pasta
    (or penne)
300g/10½oz sprouting broccoli, cut into
    chunks (stalks discarded)
freshly grated Parmesan, dried chilli flakes
    and extra virgin olive oil, to serve

Cook the sausage mixture as outlined above, then stir in the rosemary.

Meanwhile, bring a large pan of salted water to the boil. Add the pasta and bring back to a boil, then add the broccoli and cook until the pasta is al dente, according to the package instructions.

Drain the pasta and broccoli into a colander and tip into the pan with the sausages. Mix together, breaking up the broccoli as you go. Check the seasoning and serve topped with freshly grated Parmesan, a pinch of chilli flakes and a drizzle of olive oil.

'Bife Ana'
(Eagle-style Seared Kid Sandwich)

The best cooking job I ever had was at the Eagle in Farringdon Road, which opened its doors 26 years ago as the first 'gastropub', a term coined by Charles Campion. It has barely altered since, and its influence on British food cannot be overstated – it transformed the way we British cook and eat. The menu changes every day, but the one constant has been the 'Bife Ana' steak sandwich. Here is my homage to the Eagle and its lovely owner Mike Belben.

Make sure your pan is very hot to cook the meat.

Serves 4

600g/1lb 5oz kid neck fillet or boneless
   leg steaks
salt

for the marinade

1 onion, thinly sliced
1 bay leaf, crushed
1 garlic clove, thinly sliced
½ teaspoon dried chilli flakes
1 tablespoon chopped fresh parsley

1 teaspoon dried oregano
2 tablespoons red wine
3 tablespoons olive oil
freshly ground black pepper

to serve

4 large crusty rolls (the bigger they are
   the less juice ends up on your clothes!)
lettuce leaves

Mix together all the marinade ingredients, add the fillet and marinate in the fridge for a few hours (but no longer than 8 hours).

Remove the meat from the marinade then strain the marinade and set the liquid and onion mixture aside. Season the meat with salt.

Warm the rolls in an oven or under the grill, then cut in half.

Fry the fillet in a very hot, heavy-based frying pan for about 1–2 minutes on each side. Remove from the pan and add the onion mixture from the marinade to the pan with a pinch of salt. Fry for 1 minute, then add the liquid marinade and let it reduce to a syrup, then pour it over the top halves of the rolls.

Put the lettuce leaves on the bottom half of the rolls, slice the fillet and lay it on top then close and serve immediately.

Simple Burger

Serves 4

½ cucumber, peeled and thinly sliced
2 tablespoons Dijon mustard
1 tablespoon chopped rosemary leaves
2 tablespoons softened butter
800g/1¾lb minced (ground) kid
    (preferably shoulder)
1 tablespoon vinegar
pinch of sugar
salt and freshly ground black pepper

To serve

4 burger buns, halved
1 small red onion, thinly sliced
small bunch of rocket (arugula)
mustard BBQ sauce (page 197),
    or your favourite sauce

Sprinkle the cucumber slices with a big pinch of salt and put to one side. Beat the mustard and rosemary into the butter and keep to one side.

Divide the minced meat into 4 and shape each into a burger about 1cm/½in wider than the buns, with the edges of the burger slightly thicker than the middle. Season with salt and pepper.

Squeeze the cucumber dry and mix in the vinegar and sugar.

Cook the burgers over a high heat for about 5 minutes on each side, until crispy on the outside and still pink in the middle.

Toast the buns and spread with the flavoured butter. Place the burgers in the buns, with some cucumber, red onion, rocket (arugula) and sauce, to taste.

Schnitzel

Who doesn't like meat fried in breadcrumbs? You've got to be committed to this recipe – from bashing out the meat, coating with the breadcrumbs and the frying, it's a bit of work and can be messy, but it is 100 per cent worth it for the crispy fried result.

Serve with aïoli (page 200) or even salsa verde (page 196). Add a few sprigs of hard herbs such as sage, thyme or rosemary to the butter and oil as the schnitzel cooks, if you like.

As a variation, you can add a few tablespoons of finely crushed hazelnuts to the breadcrumbs.

Serves 4

4 boneless kid leg steaks, about 2cm/¾in thick (or use boneless loin)
1 tablespoon very finely chopped sage (or rosemary)
150g/3 cups panko (Japanese bread crumbs), or other dry breadcrumbs

3 tablespoons plain (all-purpose) flour
2 eggs
2 tablespoons vegetable or olive oil
2 tablespoons butter
salt and freshly ground black pepper
lemon wedges, to serve

Using a mallet or rolling pin, flatten the steaks out between 2 sheets of cling film (plastic wrap) or greaseproof paper, to about 5mm/¼in thick.

Mix the herbs with the breadcrumbs.

Spread the flour and herby breadcrumbs out in 2 separate, shallow bowls. In a third bowl, beat the eggs with 2 tablespoons water. Season the steaks with salt and pepper, then dredge in the flour, tapping off any excess. Dip the floured schnitzel in the egg and then coat with the breadcrumbs.

In each of 2 large frying pans (or cook in two batches in one pan), heat 1 tablespoon oil and 1 tablespoon butter. When it foams, add the schnitzel and cook over a high heat until golden, about 3 minutes. Turn the schnitzel and cook for 2 minutes more. Take care not to let the butter burn, and if using one pan, wipe it out between batches.

Drain on kitchen paper and serve with lemon wedges.

Buttered Scottadito

Loosely translated from the Italian, *scottadito* means burnt fingers. Serve with salsa verde (page 196).

Serves 4

12 kid cutlets
1 tablespoon finely chopped rosemary or
  sage leaves
grated zest of 1 lemon (keep the lemon
  to serve as wedges)

2 garlic cloves, finely chopped
70g/5 tablespoons softened
  unsalted butter
salt and freshly ground black pepper
crusty bread or toast, to serve (optional)

Using a mallet or rolling pin, flatten the cutlets out between 2 sheets of cling film (plastic wrap) or greaseproof paper, to about 1cm/½in thick.

Add the herbs, lemon zest and garlic to the butter.

Season the chops with salt and pepper. Spread the flavoured butter on both sides of the cutlets and put them in the fridge for at least 30 minutes before cooking.

Heat a barbecue, grill or griddle pan, and cook the cutlets briefly on one side, then flip them over and cook the other side – the cooking time should be anywhere between 2–5 minutes on each side, depending on the heat and how you like them cooked.

Serve the cutlets piping hot, with lemon wedges and salsa verde (page 196), and some crusty bread or garlic-rubbed toast, if you like.

Saltimbocca

This is another favourite of mine; it's the intense saltiness from the fried prosciutto that does it for me. They know their stuff, those Italians.

This recipe can also be made with chops. Serve with sautéed potatoes or polenta.

Serves 4

4 boneless kid leg steaks (or loin,
    or 8 cutlets from the rack)
12 sage leaves
8 slices of prosciutto
2 tablespoons plain (all-purpose) flour
1 tablespoon olive oil

3 tablespoons unsalted butter
2 garlic cloves, unpeeled and slightly
    flattened with the side of a knife
200ml/scant 1 cup dry Marsala or
    white wine
salt and freshly ground black pepper

Using a mallet or rolling pin, flatten the steaks out between 2 sheets of cling film (plastic wrap) or greaseproof paper, to about 5mm/¼in thick. Cut each piece into 2 (unless using cutlets), stick a sage leaf to each (reserve the remaining 4 leaves) and give it a nice grinding of pepper. Wrap each steak in a slice of prosciutto and dust lightly with flour.

Heat the oil and butter in a large frying pan over a medium heat. Add the garlic and the reserved sage leaves, then add the steaks and cook for 2 minutes on each side until golden and cooked through. Remove and keep warm on a serving dish.

Add the Marsala or wine to the pan and bubble it over a high heat until thickened and reduced by half. Remove and discard the garlic cloves, taste for seasoning and serve poured over the steaks.

Ragù (from Leftovers)

Serves 4

3 tablespoons extra virgin olive oil
about 300g/10½oz leftover cooked kid,
   roughly chopped (you can use as little
   or as much as you have)
2 tablespoons tomato paste
4 garlic cloves, finely chopped
1 onion, roughly chopped
2 celery sticks, finely chopped
1 carrot, finely chopped
½ teaspoon dried chilli flakes,
   or more to taste

100ml/scant ½ cup white or light red wine
1 x 400g/14oz can whole plum
   tomatoes, drained
1 teaspoon dried oregano
400g/14oz short tube pasta, such
   as penne
small handful of green olives, pitted
   and roughly chopped (optional)
salt and freshly ground black pepper
Parmesan, pecorino or hard
   goat's cheese, grated, to serve

Heat 1 tablespoon of the oil in a frying pan, add the cooked meat and fry to brown the surfaces as much as possible. Add the tomato paste and garlic, and cook for 1 minute. Check the seasoning, adding salt and pepper to taste, and set aside.

Heat the remaining 2 tablespoons oil in a saucepan, add the vegetables and chilli flakes and fry for 10 minutes, until soft. Add the wine and cook until reduced by half, then add the tomatoes and oregano, along with a pinch of salt and pepper, and cook until thick and rich, about 30–40 minutes.

Cook the pasta until al dente, according to the packet instructions, then drain, reserving a couple of tablespoons of the cooking liquid.

Stir the meat and the olives, if using, through the sauce and add the reserved pasta cooking water, then stir the pasta through. Serve immediately, topped with grated cheese.

Liver with Cumin and Chilli

Best served with chopped salad and yoghurt sauce (page 201), and some lemon wedges to squeeze over. This one's for you, Bob Granleese.

Serves 4

600g/1lb 5oz fresh kid liver, thinly or thickly sliced (depending on how you like it cooked)

1 teaspoon ground coriander

2 teaspoons ground cumin, plus 1 extra teaspoon to serve

½ teaspoon cayenne pepper

½ teaspoon sweet smoked paprika (use unsmoked if you prefer)

½ teaspoon hot paprika

½ teaspoon dried chilli flakes

40g/3 tablespoons unsalted butter, melted (or use vegetable or olive oil)

salt and freshly ground black pepper

Put the liver slices in a bowl with the spices, ½ teaspoon salt and half the melted butter. Toss together with your hands, then cover and leave for 20 minutes.

Mix the extra teaspoon of cumin with a bit of salt and black pepper and put to one side.

Heat a large frying pan over a high heat. When it's good and hot, add the liver and sear for about 1 minute, then flip and cook for another minute or so on the other side until cooked to your liking. Add the remaining melted butter to the pan and swirl to coat.

Serve straight away with the cumin salt on the side to sprinkle at the table.

MEATBALLS

Meatballs can be grilled as described here, or also braised in a sauce. A quick braise is OK, but a longer braise, for up to an hour, will help the flavour infuse into the sauce. They are also perfect to cook a day in advance, as they will improve overnight.

Persians call them *koofteh*, Turks call them *köfte* and Arabs *kefta* – all slightly different pronunciations of the root word for the same creation, kofta, meaning 'to pummel', in reference to the technique of working the meat so much by hand that the proteins break down and the texture becomes silky-smooth.

If you like your meatballs crisp rather than soft on the exterior, flouring them before frying will achieve this.

Three Kofta Variations

These flavouring mixes also make excellent marinades for diced kid kebabs. To cook these on a BBQ, you will need wooden or metal skewers (soak wooden ones in water for about 30 minutes beforehand). They are all also very nice served with a herb salad, or chopped salad (page 201).

Serves 4
600g/1lb 5oz minced (ground) kid
1 teaspoon each of salt and freshly
    ground black pepper

Kofta

1 small onion, coarsely grated
3 tablespoons finely chopped
    flatleaf parsley
1 teaspoon dried mint
1 tablespoon baharat spice blend
    (page 196)

Turkish version

3½ tablespoons olive oil
3 tablespoons finely chopped fresh mint
1–2 teaspoons Turkish chilli flakes (try to
    find dark Urfa or red Aleppo chilli)
1 teaspoon dried mint
1 teaspoon tomato paste
1 tablespoon Turkish pepper paste (or
    use harissa and few of the chilli flakes)

Persian version

75g/2¾oz dried cranberries
    (or use sour cherries)
50g/⅓ cup pine nuts
1 egg
1 small onion, coarsely grated
2 garlic cloves, crushed
1 teaspoon ground turmeric
1 teaspoon ground cumin
3 tablespoons finely chopped
    flatleaf parsley

To serve
flatbreads (page 188)
chopped salad (page 201)
hot sauce (page 198)
yoghurt sauce (page 201)
lemon wedges

Put the minced meat in a bowl with the salt and pepper and all the ingredients from your chosen variation. Mix well, using your hands to squish and knead the ingredients together. Divide into 8 equal portions and, with wet hands, shape each piece into a thick sausage shape about 12cm/4¾in long. Thread each kebab onto a skewer. (They can also be shaped into ovals or balls and fried.)

Grill on the hottest part of a grill or barbecue, turning them as needed, until slightly charred and cooked through, 5–10 minutes. If the outside starts to burn before the inside is fully cooked, move to the cooler side of the grill.

Serve with flatbreads, chopped salad, hot sauce, yoghurt sauce and lemon wedges.

Kibbeh

Instead of being shaped and filled, kibbeh can also be layered in a tray, with the meat on the bottom and the shell on top. Cut deep slashes diagonally into the shell and bake in a hot oven for about 30 minutes.

Serves 4

2 tablespoons olive oil, plus extra
   for frying
½ large onion, finely chopped
1 garlic clove, crushed
400g/14oz minced (ground) kid
2 teaspoons pine nuts, toasted
1 tablespoon raisins, chopped
pinch of Turkish chilli flakes, or use
   another not-too-hot chilli
2 pinches of ground cinnamon, to taste
pinch of ground allspice, to taste

juice of ½ lemon
handful of flatleaf parsley, finely chopped
olive or vegetable oil, for frying
salt and freshly ground black pepper
yoghurt sauce (page 201), to serve

for the shell
80g/½ cup fine bulgur wheat
½ large onion, coarsely grated
½ teaspoon ground allspice
½ teaspoon ground cumin, toasted

For the stuffing, heat the 2 tablespoons oil in a pan, add the chopped onion and fry for 10 minutes until soft.

Meanwhile, rinse the bulgur wheat, transfer to a bowl and add 200ml/scant 1 cup boiling water. Leave for 10 minutes, then drain thoroughly.

Add the garlic to the onion and cook for 1 minute, then add half the minced meat and cook for 10 minutes until cooked through.

For the shell, put the remaining minced meat, grated onion, allspice, cumin and ¼ teaspoon salt in a food processor and blend to a paste. Add this paste to the drained bulgur and mix, using your hands, as if you are kneading dough.

Add the pine nuts and raisins to the cooked meat mixture, then add the spices, parsley and lemon juice, seasoning to taste.

Using wet hands, take a golf ball-sized amount of the bulgur mix, flatten it in your palm and press a dimple into the middle. Place a teaspoon or so of the stuffing mixture in the dimple then enclose the stuffing and form into a small oval shape. Repeat with the rest of the mixtures and chill for 20 minutes.

Shallow fry the kibbeh in oil in a frying pan, turning frequently, until they are deep brown all over. Serve with yoghurt sauce.

Sheftalia

The dripping of the caul fat onto the barbecue makes these sheftalia special, but they are also delicious grilled or fried. Caul fat is the lacy fat membrane encasing the internal organs of an animal, and is most commonly found wrapping faggots. It comes in thin sheets that are compacted together, and you can buy it from traditional butchers.

Serves 4

600g/1lb 5oz minced (ground) kid
2 tablespoons breadcrumbs
small bunch of parsley, finely chopped
small bunch of mint, finely chopped
1 onion, coarsely grated
2 garlic cloves, crushed
½ teaspoon dried oregano

1 egg, lightly beaten
1 teaspoon ground cinnamon
½ teaspoon cracked black pepper
1 teaspoon salt
juice of 1 lemon
250g/8¾oz caul fat, soaked in cold water
   for 10 minutes

Mix all the ingredients except the caul fat together, and chill for 30 minutes.

Drain the caul fat flat, lay it out flat and pat dry, then cut it into about 7cm/2¾in square pieces. Put about a tablespoon of the meat mixture in the centre of each caul fat square, fold in the outside edges and roll.

Prepare a barbecue for high heat, preheat a grill, or heat a wide frying pan. Barbecue, grill or fry the sheftalia for 10–12 minutes, turning frequently, until the outside is crispy and dark and the inside is no longer pink.

Kibbeh Nayeh

You might be tempted to use mince for this, but the texture of hand-chopped meat is so much better. Traditional recipes knead the mix to a paste, but I prefer the looser texture of a brief mix of the ingredients, like a tartare. Feel free to mix more vigorously if you prefer, or even knead to a paste.

It goes without saying that this recipe requires really fresh meat, and if you are feeling brave, fresh kid heart instead. I love this dish – its subtle, fresh, zesty flavour is the opposite of what people expect from goat meat.

Serves 4

1 small onion, very finely chopped
about 80g/½ cup fine bulgur wheat
   (or freekeh)
400g/14oz lean kid meat with no sinew
   (leg or loin is best)
juice of 1 lemon, or to taste
dried chilli flakes, black pepper and
   cinnamon, to taste (go easy on the
   cinnamon)

small bunch of fresh parsley or mint,
   finely chopped
salt

To serve

extra virgin olive oil
pine nuts, toasted (optional)
toasted flatbreads (page 188)
sweet white cabbage (optional)

Rub a big pinch of salt into the onion and put to one side.

Rinse the bulgur in cold water until the water runs clear, then soak in warm water for 30 minutes. Drain by squeezing it in your hands.

Meanwhile, finely chop the meat by hand, adding lemon juice, spices and salt to taste. Leave for 10 minutes.

Rinse the onion and dry well, then add to the meat mixture with the herbs and most of the bulgur; add more if the mixture is still quite wet. Mix well and add more salt, spices or lemon juice to taste.

Serve with a drizzle of olive oil and a few toasted pine nuts scattered over the top if you like, with a flatbread on the side. Some sweet white cabbage leaves are also nice to scoop up the meat mixture.

Cooking Kid Chops

These timings are for kid chops that are approximately 150g/5¼oz and 3cm/1¼in thick. Before cooking, get the chops out of the fridge so they can come up to room temperature. If frying, drain the meat on kitchen paper to prevent spitting when adding to the pan.

Drizzle the uncooked chops with olive oil and season with a pinch of sea salt, and rub into the meat.

In the oven

Preheat the oven to 180°C/350°F/gas mark 4 and cook in a roasting tin for about 15–20 minutes, or until cooked to your liking, turning halfway so they brown evenly.

In a frying pan or griddle

Only cook as many chops as you have room for in the pan or griddle; they shouldn't touch each other. Place a frying pan or griddle over a medium heat and, when hot, add the chops. Cook for 3–5 minutes on each side (depending on thickness), turning every minute, until coloured on both sides. Turn the chops onto the fat edge to colour for 1 minute at the end.

On the BBQ

Get the coals on the barbecue hot and glowing, without too much flame. Rake the coals into a big hot pile on one side and a smaller, cooler, pile on the other. Put the chops on the hot side without touching each other. Cook for 4 minutes, turning often, until light brown on both sides, moving them away from any flare-ups. When golden all over, move the chops to the cooler side to cook through.

Under the grill

To grill the chops, preheat the grill to high. Cook for 4–6 minutes on each side, or for chops over 2cm/¾in thick, for 6–8 minutes on each side. (These times can be used as a guide for barbecuing thicker chops too.)

After cooking, rest chops for 2–3 minutes before serving, for best results.

Mark Hix

Goat Dumplings
with Caramelised Shallots and Puy Lentils

Mark and I are from the same part of the world, near Lyme Regis in Dorset, and his restaurant perched on the hill above the Cobb has one of the best views of any restaurant anywhere in the world. Mark has always been a strong advocate of British food and small producers, and we have been grateful beneficiaries of that.

Serves 8
for the goat dumplings
6 large shallots, chopped
10g/½oz sprig of thyme, leaves finely
   chopped
1 garlic clove, peeled and crushed
30g/2 tablespoons butter
100ml/scant ½ cup red wine
500g/1lb 2oz fatty minced (ground) pork
500g/1lb 2oz boneless kid shoulder,
   minced
200g/4 cups fresh white breadcrumbs

150g/5½oz caul fat (see page 100)
salt and freshly ground black pepper

for the sauce
25–30 medium-sized shallots, peeled
2 teaspoons olive oil
30g/2 tablespoons butter
100g/½ cup Puy lentils, soaked for 1 hour
100ml/scant ½ cup red wine
500ml/2 cups good dark meat stock
1 tsp cornflour (corn starch), if needed

For the dumplings, gently cook the chopped shallots, thyme and garlic in the butter until soft, then add the red wine and simmer until reduced by two thirds. Leave to cool, then mix with the rest of the ingredients, except the caul fat, adding salt and pepper to taste. Take a small piece of the mixture and cook gently in a frying pan, then taste it to check the seasoning; adjust if necessary.

Wash the caul fat in cold water then dry on some kitchen paper. Mould the dumpling mixture into 8 evenly sized balls and wrap a couple layers of the caul fat around each. Put in the refrigerator for 30 minutes to rest.

Preheat the oven to 200°C/400°F/gas mark 6. To make the sauce, roast the shallots in a heavy roasting pan with the olive oil and butter for about 30–40

minutes, seasoning with salt and pepper halfway through cooking and stirring well so that they colour evenly.

Drain the lentils and cook in boiling, salted water for 15–20 minutes until just tender. Simmer the red wine in a pan until it has reduced by half, then add the meat stock. Continue to simmer until reduced by two thirds and beginning to thicken. If the sauce is not thickening, mix cornflour (cornstarch) with water and stir into the sauce. Mix in the lentils and roasted shallots and put to one side.

Roast the dumplings for 20 minutes in a heavy roasting pan, turning them halfway through cooking.

To serve, reheat the sauce, dry the dumplings on some kitchen paper before plating, then spoon over some sauce.

Elliott Lidstone

Loin of Goat, Cracked Wheat
and Anchovy Dressing

At the time of writing, Elliott cooks at Box E in Bristol. We got to know each other via Twitter as I kept asking/nagging/harassing him into trying our product. He eventually caved in while he was head chef at The Empress in Hackney, and the results were brilliant. There is finesse, a lightness of touch, in Elliott's cooking that marks him out, and you can see it in his contribution here.

Serves 4
about 600g/1lb 5oz kid loin
splash of vegetable oil
50g/3½ tablespoons butter
salt and freshly ground black pepper

for the anchovy dressing
1 shallot, finely chopped
1 x 50g/2oz tin of anchovies, drained
   and finely chopped
1 tablespoon white wine vinegar
3 tablespoons olive oil

for the cracked wheat
250g/9oz cracked wheat
1 leek, finely chopped
3 celery sticks, finely chopped
1 garlic clove, crushed
splash of olive oil
150g/5½oz mixed seeds (pumpkin
   and sunflower work well)
½ bunch of parsley, chopped

Preheat the oven to 200°C/400°F/gas mark 6.

For the anchovy dressing, mix the shallot and anchovies in a bowl with the vinegar and oil, ensuring that the anchovies are dispersed throughout. Set aside.

Put the cracked wheat in a large heat-proof bowl, pour over 500ml/2 cups boiling water, cover and leave for 15 minutes.

Sweat the leek, celery and garlic in a pan with the oil until tender. Mix with the cracked wheat. Toast the seeds in a dry pan and add to the cracked wheat with the chopped parsley. Mix well and season to taste.

Cut the loin into 4 equal portions and seal in a hot pan with the oil until the outside is browned. Add the butter and, when it is melted and foaming, spoon it over the loin. Transfer to the oven and cook for 4 minutes. The loin is best served pink but needs to be rested well (for around 10 minutes) in a warm place.

Heap the cracked wheat onto four plates. Slice the loin thinly and place on top. Spoon over the anchovy dressing and serve.

Hugh Fearnley-Whittingstall

Kid, Lentil and Labneh Salad
with Parsley and Dukka

I was lucky enough to work for Hugh a few years ago at the River Cottage Canteen in Axminster. That was where I first cooked and experimented with our own goat meat on the menu. Hugh's enthusiasm for food, his drive to fix some of the problems in the food industry, and his example of what can be achieved with effort were, and still are, an inspiration for Cabrito.

Labneh is a thick, creamy, fresh yoghurt cheese – a delicious partner to seared kid meat and Puy lentils. You can make your own labneh by adding salt to plain, whole milk yoghurt and draining it through muslin for a few hours.

Serves 2

50g/¼ cup Puy lentils
½ garlic clove, finely chopped
½ teaspoon English mustard
3½ tablespoons extra virgin olive oil
a good squeeze of lemon juice
300g/10½oz kid leg steak, about
    2cm/¾in thick, or kid chops
olive or rapeseed oil, for frying
2 good handfuls of flatleaf parsley leaves
150g/5½oz labneh yoghurt cheese
    (see recipe introduction)
salt and freshly ground black pepper

for the dukka

50g/2oz whole blanched almonds
    or hazelnuts
½ tablespoon cumin seeds
½ tablespoon coriander seeds
1½ tablespoons sesame seeds
½ tablespoon sunflower seeds
¼ teaspoon dried chilli flakes
¼ teaspoon flaky sea salt

Put the lentils in a saucepan, cover with cold water and bring to the boil. Reduce the heat and simmer for 10–15 minutes, until tender but still *al dente*. Drain and return to the hot pan. Add the garlic, mustard, olive oil, lemon juice and some salt and pepper, and stir well. Put the lid on the pan to keep the lentils warm.

While the lentils are cooking, make the dukka: set a dry frying pan over a medium heat, add the nuts and all the seeds and allow them to toast gently, tossing them often so they don't burn. When the nuts are lightly coloured and everything is smelling fragrant, transfer to a pestle and mortar. Add the chilli and flaky sea salt. Give the mix a good bashing but leave it nicely textured and chunky. Taste, and add more chilli and salt if you like. Set aside.

Heat a frying pan over a high heat. Rub the steak or chops with a little oil, season and lay the meat in the hot pan. Cook for about 7 minutes, turning 2 or 3 times, to render the meat nicely browned but still pink in the middle. Remove the pan from the heat but leave the meat in it to rest for a further 5 minutes.

Scatter the parsley over two plates. Spoon over the labneh and about half the lentils. Slice the meat thinly (leave chops whole) and arrange over the plates. Add the remaining lentils and any of the lovely seasoned oil left in the pan. Scatter over some of the dukka and serve.

Olia Hercules

Steamed Dumplings
Filled with Goat Meat

Olia has made dumplings cool again. This recipe gives you a dumpling base from which you can experiment. I've been lucky enough to eat Olia's food on a few occasions, and it has amazed every time.

Serves 4 hungry people
for the dough
1 large egg, lightly beaten
350g/2½ cups '00' flour, plus
   extra for dusting

groundnut oil, for greasing
a drizzle of melted butter, to serve
freshly ground black pepper

for the filling
250g/9oz boneless kid shoulder
150g/5½oz shallots, finely diced
40g/3 tablespoons goat butter
fine sea salt

For the dough, mix the egg and 150ml/²/₃ cup of water in a bowl and gradually add in the flour. Mix it well and knead it on a well-floured surface until the dough stops sticking to your hands. You should end up with firm, elastic dough. Wrap it in cling film (plastic wrap) and rest in the fridge for 30 minutes, or overnight.

Slice the meat into thin strips and then cut it across as finely as you can. Mix the meat with the shallots, then season really well with salt and mix thoroughly with your hands.

Roll the dough out into a 20–30cm/8–12in rectangle (about 2mm/¹/₁₆in thick) and cut it into twenty 8cm/3¼in squares.

Place 1 tablespoon of filling mixture in the centre of each square and add a tiny piece of goat butter on top of the filling. Pull up the two opposite edges of the square and stick them firmly together above the meat. Do the same with the two other edges, creating an X shape with the edges. Now join the 'ears' by joining the corners, turning the X shape into an infinity sign.

Lightly grease your steamer with some groundnut oil and pop the dumplings in. Steam them for 15–20 minutes or until the filling is cooked inside. Serve with a drizzle of melted butter and plenty of pepper.

Russell Brown

Kid Cutlets with a Chickpea, Pepper and Tomato Casserole

Russell and I met while he was cooking at his Dorchester restaurant, Sienna. Retaining a Michelin star in his 14-cover restaurant for five years in a kitchen the size of a broom cupboard was no mean feat – undoubtedly one of the most impressive things I've seen in cooking. The food at Sienna was faultless, as was the service from Eléna, his wife, and I miss it.

Serves 4
for the casserole
2 tablespoons olive oil
2 onions, finely diced
2 garlic cloves, thinly sliced
1 teaspoon cumin
1 teaspoon paprika
2 roasted red (bell) peppers, skinned, deseeded and diced (or use tinned or jarred)
½ x 400g/14oz can good-quality plum tomatoes
1 x 400g/14oz can chickpeas, drained (or 250g/1¾ cups cooked chickpeas)

1 tablespoon flatleaf parsley, roughly chopped
Maldon sea salt and freshly ground black pepper

for the kid
8 kid cutlets (removed from the fridge 30 minutes before cooking)
2 tablespoons olive oil
generous knob of butter
2 sprigs of thyme
250g/9oz spinach, washed

Heat 1 tablespoon of the oil in a pan with a pinch of salt, add the onions and garlic and sweat until soft, about 8–10 minutes. Add the spices and cook for a further minute. Add the diced (bell) pepper, tomatoes and chickpeas. Season well and simmer gently for 15 minutes. Adjust the seasoning and remove from the heat. Set aside.

Season the cutlets well. Heat 1 tablespoon of the olive oil in a frying pan over a medium heat, add the cutlets and fry, turning when well browned, for about 3 minutes on each side for medium rare.

Add the butter and thyme to the pan and baste the cutlets with the hot butter. Rest in a warm place for 5 minutes before serving.

Meanwhile, heat the remaining oil in a large saucepan and add the spinach, cooking until wilted. Season to taste.

To serve, reheat the chickpea casserole and stir in the remaining tablespoon of olive oil and parsley at the last minute. Divide the spinach between bowls, lay the cutlets against the spinach and spoon the casserole around.

Jonathan Woolway

Devilled Kidneys

So much has been written and said about the wonderful St John that there isn't much I can add to the praise. For me, it's the most influential British restaurant of all time, and to have our meat on the menu still gives me a thrill. This recipe is a St John classic.

Serves 2

6 kid kidneys, suet and membrane removed, split in half lengthways (retaining the kidney shape)
3 tablespoons plain (all-purpose) flour
1 teaspoon cayenne pepper
1 teaspoon English mustard powder
big knob of butter

splash of Worcestershire sauce
healthy splash of chicken stock
2 slices toast (white or brown, up to you, though – just an observation – white seems to sup up the juices better)
salt and freshly ground black pepper

Nip out the white fatty gristle of the kidneys with a knife or scissors. Mix together the flour, cayenne, mustard, and some salt and pepper in a bowl.

Get a frying pan very hot, throw in the butter and, as this melts, roll the kidneys in the spiced flour, then shake them in a sieve to remove excess. Place them in the sizzling-hot pan and cook for 2 minutes on each side. Add a hearty splash of Worcestershire sauce and the chicken stock, and let all the ingredients get to know each other.

Remove the kidneys to your two waiting bits of toast. Let the sauce reduce and emulsify in the pan (do not let it disappear), then pour it over the kidneys and toast.

Elizabeth Haigh

Goat Ragu Wonton, XO
and Burnt Cabbage

I think Elizabeth is the most exciting chef working in London. She has a unique blend of influences that give her a style all her own. This is a beautiful recipe with a mix of skills that any cook will find useful to learn.

Serves 4 (makes 35–40 dumplings)
for the goat ragu filling
1 shoulder of kid on the bone
   (about 1.5kg/3¼lb), cut into 3 pieces
   (ask the butcher to do this, or just use
   diced boneless shoulder)
60ml/¼ cup extra virgin olive oil
2 celery sticks, finely chopped
2 small carrots, finely chopped
1 onion, finely chopped
1kg/2lb 3oz canned chopped tomatoes
310ml/1¼ cups lamb stock
6 sprigs of thyme
2 fresh bay leaves
20g/1½ tablespoons butter

1 tablespoon roughly chopped
   flatleaf parsley
salt and freshly ground black pepper

for the wontons and to finish
9cm/3½in square wonton sheets
   (10 small ones per portion)
1 hispi cabbage, washed, outer
   leaves removed
50g/3½ tablespoons butter, cubed
4 tablespoons XO sauce
sesame oil and sliced spring onions
   (scallions), to garnish

Preheat the oven to 140°C/275°F/gas mark 1. Season the meat well.

Heat the oil in a flameproof casserole over a medium-high heat until smoking, add the meat and fry, turning occasionally, until browned, about 3–5 minutes. Transfer to an oven tray and keep warm.

Add the celery, carrots and onion to the casserole and sauté until starting to caramelise, 10–12 minutes. Add the tomatoes and stock and bring to the boil, then add the thyme and bay leaves.

Return the meat to the casserole, cover closely with baking paper, put a lid on and bake in the oven until the meat is tender and almost falls from the bone, 2¼–3 hours.

Remove the meat from the sauce and, when cool enough to handle, break into bite-sized pieces (discard any bones, if used). Remove the herbs from sauce and discard, then blend the sauce with a hand blender until smooth.

Return the meat to the sauce, bring just to the boil over a medium heat, then stir in the butter. Season to taste, then cool and chill.

To make the wontons, peel off a wonton wrapper and, using a pastry brush, lightly brush around the outside edge with cold water. Place 1 teaspoon of chilled ragu mixture in the centre and fold into a half-moon shape, squeezing the edges together to seal. Do not overfill. Repeat until you have around 35–40.

(These can now be chilled for up to 1 hour on a tray lined with baking parchment.)

When ready to cook, heat a large saucepan (ideally with a bamboo steamer attachment to fit on top) of salted water until boiling. At the same time, heat a cast-iron frying pan or skillet until searing hot.

Meanwhile, quarter the cabbage but keep the core in. Blanch in boiling water for 1 minute then remove and place into an ice bath straight away to prevent it over-cooking.

Place the cabbage cut side down in the hot frying pan or skillet and colour until blackened and warmed through. Cut the core off while still hot and toss the quarters with the butter, and salt and pepper to taste.

Steam the dumplings in a bamboo basket over the boiling water for 5 minutes. Carefully place into a bowl, with the XO sauce and the cabbage, garnish with sesame oil and thinly sliced spring onions (scallions) and serve immediately.

Over Fire

I am a relatively new convert to live fire cooking. Years of cooking in restaurants have meant I'm more accustomed to gas burners and ovens, but since my 'retirement' I've been able to explore barbecuing a bit. With the help of the generous and enthusiastic online BBQ community, I've added a few more skills to my cooking and a few more ovens to my garden.

Goat responds beautifully to smoke and fire. The meat is robust enough to stand up to the flavour imparted by wood and charcoal, and its sweetness offers a lovely contrast. The recipes in this chapter are a mix of the quick-barbecued with a punchy marinade, and the slow-smoked which offer the 'pulled' meat that is so juicy and delicious.

As good as the recipes are, they are only half the story. There is something about getting outside and cooking that turns a lunch or dinner into a gathering and an event. It strips away the formality of eating, making it more relaxed and convivial, be it for two people or ten. That is what I hope you do with these recipes: invite some friends round, have a cook-out, and enjoy yourself.

Five Marinades for Skewers

All these marinades can also be used for chops or other quick-cooking cuts, so please experiment! If you are using wooden rather than metal skewers, it's best to soak them in water for at least 30 minutes before using so they don't catch fire.

Makes 6–8 skewers

1 quantity of your chosen marinade (see below)

600–800g/1lb 5oz–1¾lb kid, cut into 3–4cm/1¼–1½in cubes

1 tbsp oil (if frying, not grilling or cooking on the BBQ)

salt and freshly ground black pepper

Mix whichever marinade you are using, following the method outlined, with the diced meat, and leave to marinate for at least an hour. Anything up to 24 hours (in the fridge) is fine – the meat will just take on more flavour.

Thread the marinated meat onto skewers and season with salt and pepper.

Cook over a hot barbecue, under a grill or in a griddle pan for about 3–4 minutes on each side – you want them to be just cooked through and still juicy on the inside, although they can be cooked as pink as you like.

Pinchos morunos

Pinchos morunos are inspired by Moorish cuisine, and are popular in the Andalusia and Extremadura regions of Spain. Serve the skewers with a green salad, lemon wedges, crusty bread and aïoli (page 200).

1 teaspoon hot or sweet pimentón (Spanish paprika)

1 teaspoon ground cumin

1 teaspoon dried oregano

½ teaspoon ground fennel seeds

1 garlic clove, crushed

1 tablespoon olive oil

Mix together all the ingredients in a bowl and use to marinate the diced meat.

Sichuan

Use any diced meat here, but I like diced breast for this. The spices really cut through the fat.

1 tablespoon coarsely ground toasted cumin seeds

1–2 teaspoons dried chilli flakes

1 teaspoon coarsely ground Sichuan peppercorns

1 teaspoon coarsely ground fennel seeds

1 tablespoon Shaoxing wine, sake or dry sherry (optional)

1 tablespoon vegetable oil

Mix the spices together in a bowl. Mix the diced meat with the wine, if using, and oil, then add half the spice mix. Stir to coat and leave to marinate. Sprinkle over the rest of the spice mix as the kebabs cook.

Jerk

This Caribbean-influenced marinade is probably the flavour people most associate with goat. Removing the seeds from the Scotch bonnets will reduce the heat, or you could have a cold beer to hand. Serve the skewers with hot sauce (page 198) and sweet potatoes or rice.

1 teaspoon ground allspice
1 teaspoon ground ginger
1 teaspoon ground black pepper
½ teaspoon ground cinnamon
½ teaspoon ground nutmeg
1 teaspoon dried thyme
2 fresh or dried bay leaves
½ bunch spring onions (scallions), trimmed and finely chopped
1 Scotch bonnet chilli, finely chopped (take care when handling)
1 tablespoon brown sugar
1 tablespoon dark soy sauce
juice of 1 lime
2 tablespoons rum (optional)

Put all the ingredients into a small food processor and blend to a paste. Use to marinate the diced meat.

Souvlaki

Serve wrapped in flatbreads with yoghurt sauce (page 201).

1 small bunch of thyme, leaves finely chopped
1 teaspoon sweet paprika
3 garlic cloves, crushed
50ml/3½ tablespoons red wine
50ml/3½ tablespoons olive oil
grated zest and juice of 1 lemon

Mix all the ingredients, apart from the lemon juice, in a bowl, add the diced meat, stir to coat and leave to marinate.

Before skewering, strain the meat, reserving the marinade, and mix the lemon juice into the drained marinade. Brush the skewers with the lemon juice and marinade mixture as they cook.

Mexican Chilli Citrus

This is a lovely recipe. Using fresh tomato, rather than paste or canned, is something I don't do often enough.

2 dried ancho or pasilla chillies, stemmed and deseeded
1–2 chipotle chillies (or use chipotle paste or adobo), stem and seeds removed
3 garlic cloves, unpeeled
1 tomato, halved
½ teaspoon ground cinnamon
½ teaspoon ground cumin
½ teaspoon salt
2 tablespoons vegetable or olive oil
juice of ½ small orange
juice of 1 small lime

Dry-fry all the whole chillies in a moderately hot pan for about 30 seconds until just browned and aromatic. Transfer to a bowl, cover with boiling water and set aside for about 10 minutes.

Add the garlic cloves and the tomato halves, skin side down, to the dry pan and char for 5 minutes. Remove and, when cool enough to handle, peel the garlic and tomato halves.

Drain the chillies and add to a small food processor with the charred tomato and garlic, spices and salt, and blend to a smooth paste.

Fry the paste in the oil for 10 minutes until very thick, then leave to cool a little and add the citrus juices. Allow to cool then mix with the meat and leave to marinate.

Butterflied Leg of Kid with Preserved Lemon

This recipe has it all: a bit of spice, a bit of sharpness, a bit of smoke, freshness from the herbs. It's what BBQs were made to do. Serve with flatbreads or couscous, and chopped salad (page 201).

Serves 8

1 boned leg of kid, about 1.5kg/3¼lb, butterflied (see below, or ask your butcher to do this for you)
salt and freshly ground black pepper

for the marinade
juice of ½ lemon
2 tablespoons harissa paste
2 tablespoons extra virgin olive oil
3 garlic cloves, crushed
3 bay leaves, torn

for the preserved lemon dressing
3 preserved lemons, rind only
  (discard the pulp)
4 tablespoons extra virgin olive oil
juice of ½ lemon
about 4 tablespoons finely chopped
  coriander (cilantro) and/or parsley

To butterfly the leg of kid, first place the boned leg on a board. Use a sharp knife to open out the leg following along the line of the muscles. You should see 3 distinct lines denoting the 3 muscles making up the whole leg. Cut along one of these: you want the outside meat of the leg to lie flat on the board. Cut away any excess sinew. Slash any thicker sections of muscle to give an even thickness across the whole slab of meat.

Lay a piece of cling film (plastic wrap) or parchment paper over the meat and firmly hit with a rolling pin to flatten it slightly.

Mix the marinade ingredients together in a wide dish, add the butterflied leg and turn to coat in the marinade. Season,

cover with cling film and chill overnight in the fridge (or for up to 48 hours).

Preheat the barbecue and bring the meat back to room temperature.

Put the preserved lemon rind, oil and lemon juice into a small food processor. Blend to a coarse paste then stir through the chopped herbs.

Once the coals have turned grey, cook the butterflied leg for about 10 minutes on each side for nicely pink, or for longer for more well done meat, avoiding flare-ups and scorching as much as possible. Remove from the barbecue and smear the preserved lemon dressing all over the meat. Cover with foil and leave to rest for 10 minutes before slicing to serve.

Suya Kid Chops

This Nigerian recipe is usually served as diced meat on skewers. You can add oil to the dry rub to make a marinade for the meat if you prefer, but using it as a rub really lifts the flavour and texture of the whole chops.

Serve with chopped salad (page 201) and hot sauce (page 198).

Serves 4

12 kid chops, cut quite thin
vegetable oil, for coating
salt

for the suya spice mix
50g/1¾oz roasted peanuts
25g/1oz crackers or dry breadcrumbs
½ teaspoon ground ginger

1 teaspoon dried thyme
1 stock cube, crumbled (optional)
1–2 teaspoons cayenne, dried chilli flakes or chilli powder (adding even more if you like it hot – if you can find Scotch bonnet flakes, give them a go)
1 teaspoon ground black pepper

Using a small food processor or pestle and mortar, blend or crush the peanuts and crackers or breadcrumbs with the spices and the stock cube, if using, to a fine powder.

Rub the chops with oil and a little salt then rub on three-quarters of the spiced nut mix.

Cook over medium coals, or grill or roast for about 5 minutes on each side, taking care the coating doesn't burn.

Eat straight off the grill, topped with the rest of the spiced nut mix.

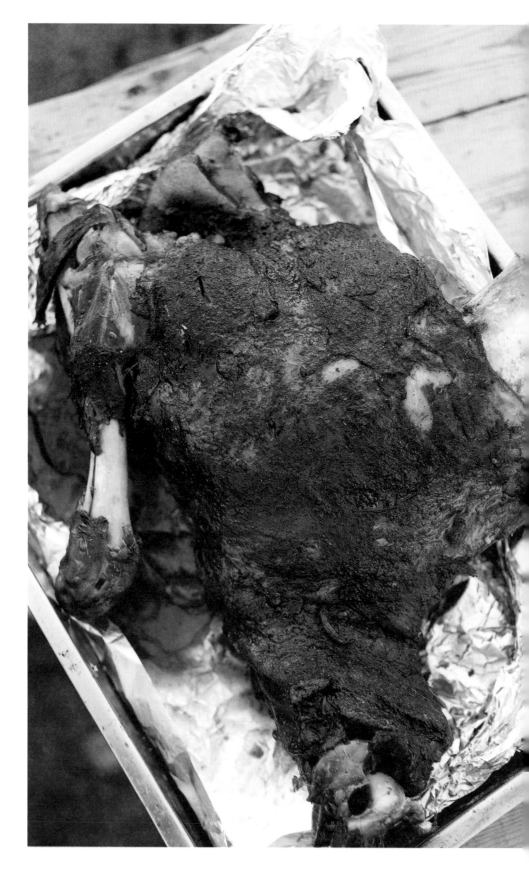

Slow Barbecue Kid Shoulder

This recipe is best cooked on a ceramic or kettle BBQ that has a temperature gauge attached (see page 140 for instructions). Throw a bit of wood in with the charcoal for the full smoky effect.

The meat can be pulled and tossed through the juices, or cut into chunks with the juices on the side as a sauce. Serve with mustard BBQ or chipotle sauce (pages 197 and 200).

Serves 8–10

1 shoulder of kid, about 2.5kg/5½lb
  bone-in weight, or boneless

for the spice paste

1 teaspoon cracked black pepper
1 teaspoon dried oregano or thyme
1 teaspoon sweet smoked paprika
1 teaspoon English mustard powder
1 teaspoon ground cumin
1 teaspoon dried chilli flakes,
  or more to taste

1 teaspoon ground allspice
1 teaspoon ground ginger
2 teaspoons salt
1 tablespoon brown sugar (or your
  favourite sweetener, such as honey,
  maple syrup, etc.)
2 tablespoons vinegar
2 garlic cloves, peeled

Put all the spice paste ingredients into a small food processor and blend to a paste. Rub over the shoulder, place in a roasting tray, cover and leave to marinate in the fridge for up to 12 hours.

Set up the barbecue or smoker for indirect cooking and preheat to around 160°C/320°F.

Uncover the roasting tray containing the meat, pour a cup of water into the base of the tray and place on the indirect side of the grill. Close the lid and smoke for around 6 hours or until meltingly tender and the bone easily slides away from the meat.

Remove from the barbecue, cover and rest for 30 minutes. Drain off any excess fat from the roasting tray and shred the meat. pouring over any remaining cooking juices before serving.

Hay Barbecue Goat

Hay was used in the past to insulate cooked foods – roasts were packed into boxes lined with hay to keep them hot when transported to outside events or to a separate kitchen. The hay gave such a lovely deep flavour that recipes were developed to capture it.
  Serve with redcurrant jelly and a green salad.

Serves 8–10

1 bone-in leg of kid, about 2.5kg/5½lb, at room temperature
1 shopping bagful of unsprayed hay
100g/scant ½ cup softened butter
3 tablespoons each of chopped fresh sage and thyme

3 garlic cloves, finely chopped
½ teaspoon cracked black pepper
1 generous glass of white wine
salt

Season the leg all over with salt and preheat the barbecue to high. Soak two-thirds of the hay in cold water for 10 minutes, then squeeze it dry. Get a high-sided barbecue cooking container ready: foil and an old baking tray or a foil tray, or construct a strong foil parcel.

Mix the butter with the herbs, garlic, pepper and a pinch of salt.

When the barbecue is ready, put the un-soaked dry hay on it, then put the leg onto a rack and place directly on top of the hay, cover the barbecue and smoke for 5 minutes (the hay will flare up and burn very quickly). Remove the leg and allow to cool slightly, while giving the barbecue a quick brush.

Using a sharp knife, prick the leg about 20 times all over, about 2cm/¾in deep. Smear with the flavoured butter, pushing it into the holes.

Put half the drained hay in your prepared barbecue container and drizzle the wine over the hay. Place the leg on top of the wine-soaked hay and put the remaining hay on top. Cover with a lid, or a double layer of foil wrapped well around the edge.

Cook the leg using indirect heat at 180°C/350°F for about 2 hours or until the internal temperature of the meat is about 65°C/150°F. Uncover and cook for about 20 minutes more, then allow to rest for 30 minutes, covered, before carving, scraping away any of the hay before carving.

Any juices from the pan can be poured off, strained and used for gravy, or used to warm through side dishes.

Asado Cross

This is more a series of steps and technique than a recipe. You can buy asados online – if you have a garden, I would highly recommend getting one. You can cook all sorts of meat and fish on them and they are a tremendous amount of fun.

Preparing the kid
You will need a whole kid splayed open and have it at room temperature. You will need to break the ribs on one side to prise the rib cage fully open. Season with salt, pepper and any spices you want before cooking.

Wiring up the kid
Use 1mm stainless steel wire and have pliers or wire cutters to hand. You can also use 2 butcher's hooks for the top. Lay the kid on a large table with the back facing up and place the cross on top of the kid so you can attach the bottom of the legs to the top section of the cross, using either wire or butcher's hooks. Attach the moveable bottom section of the cross to the bottom of the shoulders.

Height and distance
The height can vary as much as you want – obviously it will just take longer to cook the further the kid is from the fire. I go for around 50cm/20in from the fire and keep an eye on it. Too low or close and the fat can cause havoc with the fire and the outside of the meat can scorch.

Fire
Use a mix of charcoal and wood. I use oak or beech but any good dry hardwood does the job. You'll need to manage the fire but that doesn't mean standing over it for hours.

Basting
About an hour into the cook, start to brush the meat with a salty brine with lemon juice using a rosemary, sage or thyme brush (or just use a brush). Brush about every 30 minutes.

Cooking
The kid will take 4–5 hours to cook through. Test the thickest part of the leg, near the bone, with a Thermapen: the internal temperature should be about 75°C/170°F.

Gill Meller

Goat Kebabs with Peaches, Honey, Almonds and Mint

Gill is just a wonderful cook. He has an artist's eye and thoughtful approach, and there is an integrity to his cooking that comes from understanding the ingredients and a respect for where they came from.

I love this recipe. The sweetness of the peaches complements the delicate flavour of the kid beautifully. Another recipe that challenges people's assumptions of what goat meat is and how it can be eaten.

Makes 4

300g/10½oz boneless kid meat
   (leg or loin)
4 almost-ripe peaches
1 tablespoon good olive oil

2 tablespoons runny honey
2–3 tablespoons toasted flaked almonds
2 tablespoons chopped mint
salt and freshly ground black pepper

Heat up the barbecue, or preheat your grill to high. If using wooden skewers, soak 4 for 30 minutes in cold water.

Trim the meat of any sinew or membrane, using the tip of a sharp knife, and cut it into 3–4cm/1–1½in dice.

Halve and stone the peaches, then cut them into large chunks. Thread the meat and peach chunks alternately onto 4 wooden or metal skewers; you should fit 3 or 4 pieces of each onto each skewer.

Lay the kebabs on a baking tray, trickle with the olive oil and season well with salt and pepper. Place the kebabs on the barbecue or under the hot grill and cook, turning regularly, for 3–6 minutes or until the meat is just cooked through (although you can serve it pink).

Finish with a good drizzle of honey, toasted almonds and some freshly chopped mint.

Burgers with Halloumi, Red Onion Salad and Tzatziki

Christian 'DJ BBQ' Stevenson is a force of nature. He takes cooking outside to new heights every week with his YouTube videos. When we were thinking about burger recipes, there was only one person to ask...
Fresh mint leaves can be a nice addition.

Serves 4
for the burgers
600g/1lb 5oz minced (ground) kid
½ red onion, grated
1 garlic clove, crushed (optional)
2 teaspoons Urfa chilli flakes
 (or use Aleppo)
generous pinch of ground cinnamon
½ teaspoon ground cumin
generous pinch of dried mint
½ teaspoon salt

for the onions
½ red onion, thinly sliced
½ teaspoon salt
juice of 1 lemon
small bunch of flatleaf parsley,
 leaves roughly chopped
2 tablespoons olive oil

to assemble
4 slices of halloumi, sliced into
 8 x 1cm/½in pieces
1 tablespoon olive oil
4 burger-sized lettuce leaves
8 tablespoons tzatziki
4 brioche buns, halved and toasted
4 ripe tomatoes, sliced

Combine the sliced red onion with the salt and lemon juice and set aside.

In a large bowl, combine the minced meat with the grated onion, garlic, if using, spices, dried mint and salt. Mix very well to combine, kneading a little. Divide the mixture into 4 and shape each into a burger about 1cm/½in wider than the brioche buns, with the edges of the burger slightly thicker than the middle. Set aside for at least 30 minutes, to allow the flavours to mingle.

Mix the salted sliced onion with the parsley and olive oil.

When ready to cook, fry the halloumi in the olive oil for about 30 seconds each side, until golden brown and crispy (you can also grill the halloumi). Remove and set aside.

Add the burgers to the hot pan and fry for about 5 minutes on each side, until crisp on the outside and just cooked in the middle.

Build each burger with a lettuce leaf, 2 tablespoons tzatziki, then a burger, 2 pieces of halloumi, some onion and parsley salad, and some sliced tomato.

Kelly Bramil

Smoked Shoulder of Kid Goat with Berbere

You can see more of Kelly's cooking on her website: Dreaming of the Good Life. I'll leave her to talk you through her recipe:

'I was really excited when asked to put together a recipe for the book, from the perspective of UK BBQ. Kid goat meat and live fire cooking are a match made in heaven, with the flavour profiles provided by charcoal and subtle fruit woods being beautifully matched. Treat each cut in a similar way to the lamb equivalent, and it's a great way to expand your BBQ repertoire.

Shoulder of kid, like lamb, is perfectly suited for low and slow cooking on the BBQ or smoker. When it came to deciding on flavours for this dish, it seemed a happy coincidence that I had been given some authentic berbere spice mix by my Ethiopian neighbour, so I decided it would be apt to incorporate it into this recipe. Most supermarkets now carry berbere, which packs a real punch, however the quantity used here will suit the whole family. Add more if you like it spicy!

I like to serve the shoulder shredded on a platter, sprinkled with pomegranate seeds and fresh coriander (cilantro) and accompanied by flatbreads, fresh salad leaves and a coriander, mint and yoghurt dressing. Perfect for sharing.

A note on cooking: A large kettle BBQ with a lid thermometer and top and bottom vents can be easily set up for an indirect, low temperature cook as follows:

Load one side of the fuel grate with unlit, good quality natural charcoal briquettes or lumpwood. Add about 9 or 10 lit briquettes to one side of the unlit pile and it will ignite them, acting like a fuse, and gradually burn at a low heat over a long period of time. This is known as the "minion method". The cooking grate is then put in place and the food positioned on the opposite, cooler side of the grill. The temperature is then controlled by using the vents on the BBQ. Limit the amount of air taken in through the lower vent and the temperature will decrease, and vice versa. If you own a smoker, the chances are that you are well accustomed to fire control, but the principle is essentially the same.'

Serves 6–8
500g/2½ cups plain full-fat yoghurt
1½ tablespoons berbere spice mix
    (or more to taste)
3 large garlic cloves, very finely chopped
thumb-sized piece of ginger, grated
juice of 1 lemon
1 teaspoon salt
1 shoulder of kid on the bone, about
    2kg/4½lb
2 large red onions, finely sliced

for the herby yoghurt dressing
2 heaped tablespoons chopped fresh
    coriander (cilantro), plus extra to serve
1 heaped tablespoon chopped fresh mint
juice of ½ lemon
250g/1¼ cups plain yoghurt
salt and freshly ground black pepper

to serve
pomegranate seeds
flatbreads (page 188)
salad leaves

Make a marinade by combining the yoghurt, berbere, garlic, ginger, lemon juice and salt, and mix together well. Place the shoulder in a roasting tray and spread the marinade over all sides of the meat. Lift the joint and place the sliced onions underneath, resting the meat on top. Cover and place in the fridge overnight.

Combine all the ingredients for the herby yoghurt dressing, with salt and pepper to taste, cover and set aside in the fridge for at least a couple of hours.

Set up the barbecue or smoker for indirect cooking and preheat to around 150°C/300°F. Once up to temperature, add 2 or 3 chunks of cherry wood, or another subtle smoking wood, onto and near the lit fuel.

Uncover the roasting tray containing the meat, pour a cup of water into the base of the tray and place on the indirect side of the grill. Close the barbecue lid and smoke for around 6 hours or until meltingly tender and the bone easily slides away from the meat.

Remove the meat from the barbecue, cover and rest for 30 minutes while you prepare the accompaniments.

Drain off any excess fat from the roasting tray and shred the meat, mixing it together with the now softened and caramelised onions. Sprinkle with pomegranate seeds and chopped coriander (cilantro) and stuff into flatbreads along with salad leaves and drizzle with the herby yoghurt dressing.

Roast

When it comes to food, a roast means sharing. In fact, if you are like me, food means sharing. It's one of the things I like most about it – the simple generosity in giving or receiving food. The following recipes are all about that: large cuts of meat for the centre of a table full of wine glasses, cutlery and noise.

Roasts also mean leftovers, and any of these cuts can be dropped into the sauces of the curries and slow cooks from the previous chapters to make an easy dinner.

Boned Shoulder
Stuffed with Spiced Rice

You can replace the lemon zest and juice with orange if you like. This is also good served with lightly steamed spring greens and some seasoned yoghurt mixed with fresh dill.

Serves about 8

50g/3½ tablespoons butter
½ cinnamon stick
6 green cardamom pods
150g/5½oz basmati rice, washed
    and rinsed
20g/¾oz chopped almonds, pine nuts
    or pistachios
20g/¾oz raisins, dried cherries or dried
    apricots, roughly chopped

1 small carrot, peeled and coarsely grated
small pinch of saffron strands,
    soaked in 3 tablespoons boiling water
finely grated zest and juice of 1 lemon
1.5kg/3lb 5oz boneless kid shoulder
2 tablespoons vegetable or olive oil
1 large onion, roughly chopped
salt and freshly ground black pepper

Heat the butter in a large pan, add the cinnamon and cardamom and fry for 2 minutes. Add the rice, nuts and dried fruit and stir to coat, then cook for 1 minute. Add the carrot and cook for 1 minute more, then add 250ml/1 cup water, ½ teaspoon salt and the saffron and its soaking liquid. Cover and cook for 12 minutes, then add the lemon zest and juice, and check the seasoning. Set aside.

Preheat the oven to 220°C/425°F/gas mark 7.

Open up the shoulder skin-side down on a board and trim and flatten it to open it out as much as possible. Spoon as much rice filling as will fit into the boned shoulder, reserving the rest for later. Roll up, tie with butcher's string to secure and put into a roasting dish. Rub with the oil and season with salt and pepper, then roast in the oven for 35 minutes.

Turn the heat down to 180°C/350°F/gas mark 4, give the meat a baste, then add the onion and 200ml/scant 1 cup water to the dish and roast for about a further 2 hours.

Add the remaining cooked rice to the dish, around the meat, and cook for a further 30 minutes until the rice begins to brown and crisp up and the shoulder is completely tender.

Remove from the oven and let it rest for 10 minutes, loosely covered with foil, before serving in thick slices with the rice.

Leg Wrapped in Vine Leaves

Kid legs can be wrapped in big bunches of rosemary, bay or hay if you have access to large quantities, then cooked in a similar way to this, either boned and stuffed or on the bone.

Serves 6–8

1 boned leg of kid, butterflied
   (see page 127 or ask your butcher
   to do this for you)
about 25 pickled vine leaves, rinsed
   and patted dry, stems removed
2 teaspoons dried Greek oregano
4 roasted red (bell) peppers
200g/7oz feta or halloumi
2 carrots, finely chopped
1 onion, finely chopped
400ml/generous 1½ cups kid or

chicken stock (or use water)
squeeze of lemon juice, to taste
salt and freshly ground black pepper

for the marinade

3 tablespoons olive oil
50ml/3½ tablespoons red wine
finely grated zest and juice of ½ lemon
3 bay leaves
2 sprigs of rosemary, roughly chopped
3 garlic cloves, finely chopped

For the marinade, mix the olive oil, wine, lemon zest and juice, bay, rosemary and garlic in a large dish. Add the butterflied leg and turn to coat, then cover and marinate for at least 2 hours in the fridge, or preferably overnight. Bring up to room temperature before cooking.

Preheat the oven to 190°C/375°F/gas mark 5.

Remove the meat from the marinade and pat dry, reserving the marinade. Place a large piece of foil (enough to roll the leg in) shiny side up on your work surface and place the vine leaves in a layer over the foil, rib-side up and slightly overlapping each other.

Season both sides of the meat with salt and pepper, sprinkle over the dried oregano and place the meat skin side down on top of the vine leaves. Lay the roasted red peppers along the length of the leg and crumble or coarsely grate the cheese over the red peppers.

Pull up the bottom end of the foil and vine leaves and fold over to form a

rolled, stuffed leg. Tuck the meat under to form a sealed roll and squeeze the foil around the meat. Twist the ends of the foil to tighten around the rolled leg, and tighten as much as possible.

Place in a roasting tray with a splash of water and roast in the oven for 1¼ hours, adding a bit more water if the liquid dries out. Remove the roasting tin from the oven and carefully open the foil to reveal the rolled leg. Add the carrots, onion, stock and reserved marinade to the roasting dish, and put the leg, on its foil, on top. Return to the oven for 15 minutes so that the vine leaves crisp up.

Transfer the meat to a plate to rest for 10 minutes and return the vegetables and juices to the oven. Discard the foil and vine leaves.

Adjust the seasoning of the vegetables with salt, pepper and lemon juice, then spoon onto a plate and serve topped with thick slices of the meat.

Slow-roast Baharat Shoulder

Serve, shredded, with flatbreads (page 188), chopped salad and yoghurt sauce (page 201) and zhug (page 197).

You can pretty much use any spice blend from the Mediterranean or Levant, or just make up your own!

Serves about 8

4 garlic cloves, crushed
grated zest and juice of 1 lemon
4 tablespoons baharat spice blend
   (page 196)

2 tablespoons olive oil
2 teaspoons salt
1 shoulder of kid, about 2kg/4½lb
1 large red onion, thickly sliced

In a bowl, mix together the garlic, lemon zest and juice, baharat spices, olive oil and salt.

Place the shoulder in a deep roasting tray and then rub the marinade all over. Cover and marinate in the fridge for at least 2 hours, or preferably overnight. Bring up to room temperature before cooking.

Preheat the oven to 150°C/300°F/gas mark 2.

Uncover the meat and add 250ml/1 cup water and the sliced onion to the tray. Cover the meat with baking parchment and cover the tray tightly with foil.

Roast in the oven for about 5 hours, until completely tender and the meat can be pulled off with a spoon, uncovering it for the final hour to colour the meat.

Serve the shoulder pulled or cut into chunks, with any cooking juices and the onions spooned over.

Zab

Zab is the name given to a Somali dish of roast goat served over a bed of rice; it is usually served at weddings or parties of the same name.

Serves 6–8

2 garlic cloves, crushed
2 tablespoons finely grated fresh ginger
1 teaspoon ground cumin
1 teaspoon ground coriander
½ teaspoon ground cardamom
½ teaspoon cracked black pepper
2 tablespoons vegetable oil

2kg/4½lb bone-in kid (shanks are perfect), cut into very big chunks
1 (bell) pepper (green or red), deseeded and roughly chopped
1 onion, roughly chopped
1 carrot, roughly chopped
salt

Mix the garlic, ginger, spices, half the oil and 1 teaspoon salt in a large bowl or dish, add the meat and turn to coat. Cover and marinate in the fridge for at least 2 hours, or preferably overnight. Bring up to room temperature before cooking.

Preheat the oven to 180°C/350°F/gas mark 4.

Transfer the meat to a roasting tray or large ovenproof pot with the remaining oil, and cover with a tightly fitting lid or foil. Cook gently for 30 minutes on the stovetop over a low heat, shaking the tray every now and then to stop the meat sticking, but allowing it to begin to colour.

Transfer the dish to the oven and roast, still covered, for a further 2¼ hours or until the meat is tender. Remove the lid or foil, add the vegetables and cook for a further 30 minutes, until the vegetables are tender and the meat is falling off the bone, adding a little bit of water if it dries out.

Crying Leg Boulangère

Some sliced swede (rutabaga) or turnip would be a nice addition to the potato here. This is also the method for a simple roast joint of kid, just cooking without the onion and potato, adding traditional roasted potatoes or whatever sides you like. Serve with salsa verde (page 196).

Serves 4

2kg/4½lb bone-in leg of kid
  (about ½ a full leg)
3–4 garlic cloves, sliced
big bunch of rosemary or thyme,
  roughly chopped
50g/3½ tablespoons softened butter,
  or use 3½ tablespoons olive oil

600g/1lb 5oz waxy potatoes,
  peeled and thinly sliced
2 large onions, thinly sliced
400ml/generous 1½ cups chicken
  or kid stock (or use water)
salt and freshly ground black pepper

Preheat the oven to 200°C/400°F/gas mark 6.

Rub salt and pepper all over the leg. Using a pointed knife, pierce small, deep slits about 5cm/2in apart all over the leg, inserting a slice of garlic and small sprigs of herb deep into each slit.

Place the leg in a deep roasting dish and smear the softened butter or olive oil all over the leg. Roast for 20 minutes.

Meanwhile, place the potatoes and onions in a bowl, toss together and season with salt and pepper, adding any leftover garlic and chopped herbs.

Take the meat out of the oven after its initial 20 minutes, transfer to a large plate and turn the oven temperature down to 180°C/350°F/gas mark 4.

Spread the potatoes and onions out in the roasting dish and pour over the stock, then put the leg back on top so that it is 'crying' over the vegetables.

Return the dish to the oven and roast for about another 45–60 minutes, depending on how well you like your meat cooked.

Allow the meat to rest on a plate, and meanwhile crank the oven up to crisp the potatoes a bit, if you like.

Matambre

The veg can be cut into strips and laid lengthways if you want that decorative chequer-board 70s look! This can also be slow cooked on a BBQ. Serve with chimichurri (page 198).

Serves 4

2 tablespoons olive oil
3 garlic cloves, crushed
2 tablespoons red wine vinegar
1 boned breast of kid (or use ½ a boned
   shoulder, thinly butterflied into
   flat slabs – see page 127)
1 onion, finely chopped
1 red (bell) pepper, deseeded and
   finely chopped

1 carrot, coarsely grated
bunch of parsley or oregano,
   finely chopped
4 hard-boiled eggs, peeled
handful of pitted green olives
   (or use black olives, or even capers)
sprinkling of grated cheese
   (Cheddar, feta or Parmesan)
salt and freshly ground black pepper

Mix the olive oil, garlic, vinegar and some salt and pepper in a large dish. Add the meat and marinate in the fridge for at least 2 hours, or overnight.

Preheat the oven to 180°C/350°F/gas mark 4.

Lay the meat out on a work surface and cover in the vegetables and fresh herbs. Lay the eggs lengthways along the meat, and lay the olives alongside in rows. Sprinkle over the cheese, season with salt and pepper and roll the meat lengthways away from you to form a thick roll.

Tie with butcher's string at 5cm/2in intervals to secure.

Place the roll in a roasting dish and add a splash of water to the dish. Cover and roast for about 1½–2 hours until tender, then uncover and roast for a further 15 minutes to colour.

Serve hot from the oven in thick slices with any cooking juices spooned over, or at room temperature. You can even pop it in the fridge and serve cold slices. It's a fabulous sandwich filling!

Twice-Cooked Kid with Hummus

Serve with flatbreads and zhug (pages 188 and 197) or harissa (page 199).

Serves 4

for the hummus

1 x 400g/14oz can chickpeas (garbanzo beans), drained and rinsed (or use cooked, see page 49)
1 garlic clove, peeled but left whole
3 tablespoons tahini
juice of ½ lemon
salt and freshly ground black pepper

for the spiced lamb

2 tablespoons olive oil
1 onion, finely chopped
400g/14oz leftover slow-cooked kid, chopped into small bite-sized pieces (or use minced kid, fried for 10 minutes)

2 teaspoons baharat spice blend (page 196), or use whatever Middle Eastern spice blend you like
½ teaspoon salt, or more to taste
4 tablespoons pine nuts or flaked almonds, toasted
4 tablespoons raisins, soaked in warm water for 10 minutes then drained (optional)
squeeze of lemon juice
small bunch of parsley or mint (or a mix), finely chopped
extra virgin olive oil
dried chilli flakes, to serve (optional)

For the hummus, put the chickpeas (garbanzo beans), garlic, tahini and 75ml/5 tablespoons water in a blender and process until smooth. Adjust the seasoning, adding salt, lemon juice and pepper to taste (tinned chickpeas have varying levels of saltiness). Add more water to thin the hummus to the consistency of a thick spreadable sauce and use the back of a spoon to spread hummus onto a plate.

Heat the olive oil in a pan, add the onion and fry over a high heat for 5 minutes or until softened and browning. Add the meat, spices and salt and fry until until browned, about 5 minutes.

Add the pine nuts or almonds and the drained raisins, and toss together to warm through, checking the seasoning and adding a squeeze of lemon juice.

Spoon the meat over the hummus and scatter over the parsley or mint. Drizzle over a little olive oil and add a sprinkling of chilli flakes, if using.

Kleftiko

Serves 4

1.5–2kg/3¼–4½lb bone-in shoulder of
 kid, or use a combination of shank
 and breast
800g/1¾lb medium-sized waxy potatoes,
 peeled and halved

for the marinade
juice of 1 lemon
2 tablespoons olive oil
40ml/2½ tablespoons red or white wine
4 garlic cloves, peeled but left whole
1 tablespoon dried oregano
1 teaspoon ground cumin
½ teaspoon ground cinnamon
½ teaspoon dried chilli flakes, or to taste
1 teaspoon salt, or to taste

In a small food processor, blend the lemon juice, olive oil, wine, garlic, oregano, cumin, cinnamon, chilli flakes and salt. Pour this marinade over the meat and massage well to coat all over. Cover and marinate in the fridge for at least 2 hours, or preferably overnight. Bring up to room temperature before cooking.

Preheat the oven to 230°C/450°F/gas mark 8.

Place the meat and its marinade in a roasting tray or large ovenproof pot and cover with a tightly fitting lid or foil. Roast in the oven for 20 minutes then reduce the heat to 150°C/300°F/gas mark 2 and roast for a further 1½ hours.

Lift the meat out to make room for the potatoes; there should be a good couple of centimetres/nearly an inch of liquid. If not, add a little splash of water. Add the potatoes to the tray and reposition the meat on top of the potatoes. Cover well again and continue baking for another 45–60 minutes, until the meat is completely tender and the potatoes are meltingly soft.

Remove the lid or foil, increase the oven temperature to 180°C/350°F/gas mark 4 and cook for a further 15 minutes to colour the meat and potatoes. Remove from the oven and serve.

Leftover Kid, Anchovy,
Bitter Leaf and Celery Salad

Refried chunks or slices of cold leftover roasted kid, especially slow-roasted shoulder or breast, are delicious with a salad of thinly sliced celery stalks (pale stalks only), celery leaves, chopped flatleaf parsley, puntarelle or endive leaves and a dressing made with extra virgin olive oil, lemon juice, chopped anchovies and dried chilli flakes. Fry the meat until crisp on the outside and soft in the middle.

Serves 4

½ head of puntarelle, endive or radicchio
½ celery heart, stalks finely sliced and
   leaves reserved
1 tablespoon olive oil
½ a leftover cooked kid breast, sliced into 4
4 tablespoons breadcrumbs, toasted
   (preferably from a spelt loaf)

for the dressing

1 tablespoon capers, rinsed, drained and
   finely chopped
6 anchovy fillets, roughly chopped
juice and zest of ½ lemon
1 garlic clove, peeled and finely chopped
1 tablespoon red wine vinegar
½ teaspoon dried chilli flakes
4 tablespoons olive oil
salt and freshly ground black pepper

Fill a bowl with very cold water. Pull the hollow buds from the puntarelle heads and slice very thinly lengthways. Place in the water to crisp and curl up for 1 hour. Add the celery leaves then make the dressing.

To make the dressing, in a bowl mix together the capers, anchovies, lemon juice and zest, garlic, vinegar and chilli flakes. Season to taste with salt and pepper (it should be quite salty already). Allow to sit for about 10 minutes so that the flavours meld together, then stir through the olive oil.

Heat the 1 tablespoon olive oil in a frying pan over a medium-high heat. Fry the goat pieces, stirring regularly, until deeply caramelised and crisp on all sides. Remove from the heat.

To assemble, place the warm meat on a serving platter. Drain the puntarelle and celery and mix with the dressing. Place the dressed salad on top of the meat and then top with a scattering of toasted breadcrumbs.

Jar Kitchen

Herb-crusted Rack of Kid with
Hummus, Portobello and Spiced Chickpeas

Tucked away at the top of Drury Lane in London's Covent Garden is the lovely little restaurant Jar Kitchen. Jar Kitchen is owned and run by two friends, Lucy Brown and Jenny Quintero, who made the 'brave' decision to quit their jobs in 2015 and open a restaurant because, well… they just liked restaurants. I'm very pleased they did because Jar Kitchen is fantastic.

Serves 4

2 x 6-cutlet racks of kid
extra virgin olive oil, for cooking
2 nice big portobello mushrooms
2 garlic cloves, finely chopped
small bunch of flatleaf parsley,
    leaves finely chopped
rosemary sprigs, to garnish

for the hummus
100g/¾ cup cooked chickpeas
    (garbanzo beans), drained
2 tablespoons plain yoghurt
2 teaspoons lemon juice

1 garlic clove
1 heaped tablespoon tahini
1 tablespoon extra virgin olive oil

for the spiced chickpeas
vegetable oil, for deep-frying
30g/¼ cup cooked chickpeas, drained
garam masala, to taste

for the herb crust
3 tablespoons breadcrumbs
2 teaspoons finely chopped rosemary
salt and freshly ground black pepper

Put all the hummus ingredients except the olive oil into a blender, add salt and pepper to taste and process to a nice, smooth paste. Add the olive oil and blend until emulsified. Transfer to a bowl and set aside.

For the spiced chickpeas, heat the oil in a deep fat fryer to 150°C/300°F. If you don't have a deep fat fryer, add a 6cm/2½in depth of oil to a deep, cast-iron pan and keep an eye on it. Test the oil temperature by adding a piece of bread; if it starts to spit and fry it's ready. Deep-fry the chickpeas (garbanzo beans) for 5 minutes, until crisp. Remove from the hot oil to a bowl, add garam masala, salt and pepper to taste, and set aside.

Preheat the oven to 220°C/425°F/gas mark 7.

For the herb crust, mix the breadcrumbs and rosemary with salt and pepper to taste, and add just enough olive oil to make a paste. Use your hands to pack the mixture onto the fatty part of the rack, making a nice herb crust.

Heat a little oil in a frying pan, add the rack, herb crust side down to start with. Sear, turning until golden brown on all sides. Transfer to an oven tray and roast in the oven for 8–15 minutes, depending on how you like your meat (we like to cook our rack rare).

Rest in a warm place for about 4 minutes (resting time is usually half the cooking time, and is important for all the juices to remain in the meat rather than bleeding onto the plate).

While the meat is resting, wipe the mushrooms and cut each in half, then cut each half into 3 triangular pieces. Stir-fry the garlic in some olive oil until golden, then add the mushrooms, season well, and stir-fry over a very high heat until nicely coloured. Add the chopped parsley and set aside.

To serve, spread some hummus across each plate, making a bed for the meat. Divide the rack into cutlets and put them in the middle of the plate with the bones pointing upwards to create height. Place the mushrooms around and on top of the cutlets. For the final touch, sprinkle the spiced masala chickpeas all over the plate and add a sprig of rosemary. Delicious!

Scott Goss

Kid Saddle with Black Pudding,
Clams and a Wild Garlic Crumb

Boned and rolled saddle has artistry to it. It is a real skill to prepare (you can ask your butcher to do it for you) and it makes the final dish on the plate look beautiful. This recipe, with its 'surf and turf' element and blend of colour, is a cracker and well worth the effort.

Serves 8 or a hungry 6

1 boned saddle of kid (ask your butcher to separate the fillets from the saddle)
200g/7oz good-quality black pudding, crumbled
200g/7oz spinach, wilted and squeezed dry
splash of rapeseed oil
a few garlic cloves and a couple of carrots and celery sticks, for roasting the saddle
salt and freshly ground black pepper

for the clams

500g/1lb 2oz small clams, preferably palourde, soaked in cold water for 1 hour

1 banana shallot, finely diced
30g/2 tablespoons unsalted butter
25g/1oz wild garlic, finely chopped, or 1 large garlic clove, crushed
175ml/¾ cup dry white wine

for the crumb and oil

oil for deep-frying
200g/7oz basil
100g/3½oz small wild garlic leaves
100g/3½oz brioche, stale (or dried out in a low oven)
100ml/scant ½ cup rapeseed oil

Preheat the oven to 180°C/350°F/gas mark 4.

Open flat the boned saddle. Season well and cover with the black pudding and the spinach. Place the kid fillets on top (over their original places on the saddle), roll and tie at intervals with butcher's string to secure.

Sear the rolled joint in a medium-hot pan with a little rapeseed oil until golden all over. Place the garlic cloves, carrot and celery in a roasting tray and place the seared joint on top.

Roast for 18 minutes for medium-rare, or 25 minutes for medium. Remove from the oven and rest for the same amount of time as in the oven.

Meanwhile, heat the oil for deep-frying in a deep fat fryer to 180°C/350°F. If you don't have a deep fat fryer, add a 6cm/2½in depth of oil to a deep, cast-iron pan and keep an eye on it. Deep-fry the basil and wild garlic for 30 seconds. They will spit so be careful. Lift out with a slotted spoon and drain on kitchen paper.

In a food processor, blitz half the deep-fried basil and wild garlic with the brioche into crumbs. Blitz the remaining half of the basil and wild garlic with the rapeseed oil, then strain through a muslin cloth.

Scrub the soaked clams and throw away any with broken shells. Sauté the shallot in the butter over a low heat until soft, then add the wild garlic. Increase the heat to medium-high and throw in the clams and white wine. Cook with the lid on for a few minutes until the shells have opened.

To serve, slice the meat, arrange on a platter, family style, and top with the clams still in their shells and the garlic wine liquor from the pan (leave the last few tablespoons of liquor as it might have sediment). Dress with the crumbs and oil and serve.

I like to serve this with warm buttered Jersey Royals, spring peas and asparagus, with a little fresh mint stirred through.

Baked

This chapter offers another set of recipes that are meant for the table, and for sharing. It also contains two of my favourites in the book: moussaka, thanks to my sister, and cassoulet, thanks to my friend Isobel. Isobel once cooked me a cassoulet so delicious that I've been chasing after that flavour in mine ever since. Sadly I don't have her talent so I am yet to get there!

These are forgiving recipes. They will take a bit of improvising, so as long as you follow the methods you can play with the flavours, which is a great way of developing your own style and favourites. They will also freeze very well, so making a large batch and freezing what is left is a good way of having your own range of ready meals for when you can't be bothered to cook from scratch.

Kid Biryani

I used to be a bit scared of biryanis. They always seemed complicated, but once you've got the hang of the method, you can knock them out in no time, and there are lots of different kinds to try. This can be a meal in itself or part of a larger spread.

Serves 4

75g/⅓ cup plain yoghurt,
  plus extra to serve
1½ teaspoons garam masala
1½ teaspoons curry powder (hot or mild)
2 garlic cloves, finely chopped
600g/1lb 5oz diced kid meat
2 tablespoons vegetable oil
2 medium onions, finely sliced
2 small cinnamon sticks
3 whole cloves
2 bay leaves
1 teaspoon cumin seeds
40g/3 tablespoons butter

1 teaspoon ground turmeric
350g/2 cups basmati rice
200ml/7fl oz whole milk
small bunch of coriander (cilantro),
  roughly chopped
1 fresh green chilli, finely sliced (optional)
50g/1¾oz flaked almonds, toasted
salt

to serve
1 lemon, cut into wedges
chilli and garlic chutney (page 199)

Preheat the oven to 180°C/350°F/gas mark 4.

Mix the yoghurt with the garam masala, curry powder, garlic and ¼ teaspoon of salt. Add the diced meat, turn to coat and set aside to marinate for at least 1 hour or overnight.

Heat the oil in a frying pan, add the onions and fry for about 15 minutes until soft and starting to brown. Add the marinated meat and cook for 10 minutes.

In a saucepan, fry the cinnamon, cloves, bay leaves and cumin seeds in half the butter for 1 minute over a moderate heat. Add the turmeric and rice and toast in the butter and spices for 1 minute more.

Add 450ml/15fl oz hot water and a generous pinch of salt, bring to the boil and cook, uncovered, for 5 minutes until all the water has been absorbed. Remove from the heat and add the milk.

Spread the meat and onion mixture out over the base of an ovenproof casserole which has a tightly fitting lid and pour the part-cooked rice over the top. Dot with the rest of the butter, cover tightly with the lid and cook in the oven for 1 hour.

Remove from the oven and sprinkle with the chopped coriander (cilantro), the chilli, if using, and the toasted almonds.

Serve with a few lemon wedges, some extra yoghurt and chilli chutney.

Lahmacun

In winter, replace the tomato and lemon with pomegranate molasses and toasted pine nuts. I love to roll up the lahmacun with the salad inside.

Serves 4

for the dough

500g/3½ cups strong white bread flour, plus extra for dusting
1 teaspoon fast-action dried yeast
1 teaspoon salt
olive oil, for oiling

for the topping

1 onion, chopped
2 tomatoes, chopped
1 small red (bell) pepper, deseeded and finely chopped
1 tablespoon olive oil

1 teaspoon tomato paste
1 teaspoon dried chilli flakes (preferably Turkish)
1 teaspoon ground cumin
pinch of ground cinnamon
½ teaspoon salt
250g/9oz minced (ground) kid

to serve

1 lemon, cut into wedges
large bunch of parsley, leaves only
4 large ripe tomatoes, thinly sliced

For the dough, put the flour, yeast and salt in a big mixing bowl and mix in 300ml/1¼ cups of water with a spoon. Mix well to combine completely, place a damp cloth over the bowl and leave for an hour or so until almost doubled in size.

Put all the topping ingredients apart from the minced meat into a food processor or blender and blend to a coarse paste. Don't make it too smooth. Add to the minced meat in a bowl, mix well and set aside.

When the dough is ready, preheat the oven to its maximum, with a pizza stone or baking tray inside to preheat. Turn the dough out onto a lightly floured surface and knead it gently with lightly oiled hands for 1 minute.

Cut the dough into 4 pieces and shape each into a ball. On a well-floured surface, roll each dough ball into an oval; try to get it as thin as possible without tearing.

Carefully remove the pizza stone or baking tray from the oven and place on a heatproof surface. Lay a dough oval on the stone or tray and spread a quarter of the topping evenly over the dough.

Bake for 6–8 minutes until the dough is crisp and the topping is cooked, then repeat with the remaining dough and topping. Serve immediately with the lemon wedges, parsley and tomatoes.

Fatayer

This is another of the recipes that work very well on their own, or as part of a wider feast. The fatayer are so pretty that seeing them come out of the oven as little brown parcels makes the effort worthwhile.

Makes 12

1 quantity dough (page 171)
2 teaspoons nigella or sesame seeds, to sprinkle (optional)

for the filling

2 tablespoons butter
2 small onions, finely chopped
500g/1lb 2oz minced (ground) kid
200g/7oz cooked, or defrosted frozen, spinach, squeezed dry

1 teaspoon salt
4 teaspoons baharat spice blend (page 196)
50g/1¾oz pine nuts or flaked almonds, toasted
small bunch of parsley, dill or mint, finely chopped

Have the dough proved and doubled in size as outlined on page 171.

Melt the butter in a pan, add the onions and fry until soft, about 10 minutes.

Put the rest of the filling ingredients together in a bowl, then stir in the cooked onions and mix very well. Preheat the oven to 220°C/425°F/gas mark 7.

Knead the dough for a minute or so, then divide equally into 12 pieces. Divide the filling into 12 too.

On a lightly floured surface, roll each portion of dough out to a circle about 13cm/5in diameter. Take one portion of the filling and flatten it out onto a circle of dough, leaving a 2cm/¾in clear border around the edge. Brush the border with a little water.

Wrap the dough by bring up three edges to create a little pyramid – ensure you pinch the seams well to seal the dough. Brush with water and sprinkle with the seeds, if using. Repeat with the remaining dough circles and filling, and place on a baking tray. Bake for 20–25 minutes, until golden brown. Allow to cool before serving.

Kid Moussaka

My sister is a great cook. Having spent time living in Greece and Spain, she has a lovely Mediterranean style to her food. I remember being a teenager and eating my way through an entire dish of moussaka that she'd made to feed four of us, much to her annoyance. It remains one of my favourites.

Serve with a salad, dressed with salt, olive oil and lemon juice. The kid sauce can also be used to make lasagne.

Serves 4

2 large aubergines (eggplants)
4 tablespoons olive oil
1 onion, finely chopped
2 garlic cloves, finely chopped
1 teaspoon ground cinnamon
½ teaspoon ground cumin
450g/1lb minced (ground) kid (or use
    leftover roast kid)
1 x 400g/14oz can chopped tomatoes
2 teaspoons dried oregano

for the topping

400g/scant 2 cups Greek yoghurt
2 eggs, beaten
1 tablespoon cornflour (cornstarch)
120g/4oz halloumi or feta,
    coarsely grated
freshly grated nutmeg, to taste
salt and freshly ground black pepper

Preheat the oven to 180°C/350°F/gas mark 4.

Cut the aubergines (eggplants) into 1cm/½in slices, toss with 2 tablespoons of the olive oil and season with a little salt. Place on baking sheets and bake for about 20 minutes until softened and coloured at the edges. Remove and set aside.

Meanwhile, heat the remaining olive oil in a pan, add the onion and fry for about 10 minutes until soft and translucent. Add the garlic and spices and cook for 1 minute. Add the minced meat and cook until the mixture is dry and starting to colour. Add the tomatoes and most of the oregano, and bring to the boil. Lower the heat, season with salt and pepper and cook for about 30 minutes until the sauce is concentrated and thick.

While the sauce is cooking, whisk the yoghurt with the eggs and cornflour (cornstarch) in a bowl, then stir in the grated cheese with plenty of pepper and nutmeg to taste.

Arrange a third of the aubergine slices in the base of an ovenproof dish and top with half the meat and tomato sauce. Repeat, finishing with a layer of aubergine. Pour the yoghurt sauce over the top and sprinkle with the remaining oregano.

Bake in the oven for about 45 minutes until the top is golden, bubbling at the edges and with brown patches. Remove from the oven and rest for 10 or so minutes before serving (it is also delicious served at room temperature).

Kid Cassoulet

Few things in life are more comforting than a well-made cassoulet. It's very nice with a Languedoc red wine, too. You can stir the crust multiple times to thicken the whole dish, although purists may disagree.

Serves 4

3 tablespoons olive oil
2 onions, roughly chopped
6 garlic cloves, sliced
200g/7oz streaky bacon, chopped
4 kid chops or cutlets
8 kid sausages (or use 4 pork sausages)
1 x 400g/14oz can chopped tomatoes
handful of breadcrumbs
salt and freshly ground black pepper

for the beans

350g/2 cups dried white haricot (navy)
    beans, soaked overnight in cold water
2 kid shanks
1 onion, peeled and halved
1 carrot, peeled and halved
3 bay leaves
4 garlic cloves, peeled but left whole

Drain the beans and add to a large pan with the shanks, halved onion and carrot, bay and garlic. Add enough water to cover and bring to the boil. Skim off any scum that appears, turn down to a gentle simmer and cook for about 1 hour or until the beans are almost tender, making sure the beans remain covered with water.

Drain the beans and shanks, reserving the cooking liquor and discarding the onion, carrot, bay and garlic. When cool enough to handle, remove the meat from the shanks and chop into large pieces.

Preheat the oven to 140°C/280°F/gas mark 1½.

Heat the olive oil in a large frying pan, add the chopped onions and sliced garlic and cook for 10 minutes or until soft. Add the bacon, chops and sausages to the onions and cook for 5 minutes, or until just browning. Add the tomatoes with salt and pepper to taste, and cook for about 5 minutes, or until rich and thick. Stir through the shank meat.

Spread half the meat mixture in the base of a deep casserole and cover with half the beans. Add the remaining meat, then the rest of the beans. Top up with enough of the reserved bean cooking liquor to just cover.

Sprinkle over half the breadcrumbs and bake in the preheated oven for about 1 hour. Stir the crust that has formed back into the cassoulet and top with the rest of the breadcrumbs. Return to the oven for a further 1 hour until the crust is golden, increasing the temperature for the final 10 minutes if the crust needs more browning. Serve straight from the oven.

Kid, Cabbage, Bulgur Wheat
and Tomato Pilaf

If you can manage to get the bottom of the pilaf to caramelise (without burning!) you will have additional texture.

Serves 4

50g/3½ tablespoons butter
2 onions, finely chopped
2 garlic cloves, finely chopped
1 cinnamon stick
½ teaspoon ground allspice
½ teaspoon Turkish chilli flakes, plus extra for sprinkling
2 bay leaves
1 x 400g/14oz can tomatoes
400g/14oz leftover roasted or braised kid, cut into big chunks
1 small, sweet pointed cabbage, quartered and boiled for 2 minutes, then drained

300g/1¾ cups coarse bulgur wheat, soaked in water for 10 minutes, then drained
500ml/2 cups kid stock (or use chicken stock or water)
salt and freshly ground black pepper

to serve
yoghurt (or the yoghurt sauce on page 201)
small bunch of mint, dill or parsley, roughly chopped

Melt half the butter in a pan, add the onions and fry for 5 minutes, stirring occasionally, until softened. Add the garlic and cook for 2 minutes. Stir in the spices and bay, ½ teaspoon salt and the tomatoes, and cook for 10 minutes to thicken.

In a large pan, fry the cooked meat and cabbage in the remaining butter until just coloured, then add the drained bulgur wheat. Add the tomato mixture with the stock, bring to the boil, cover and simmer gently over a low heat for 15–20 minutes, until the bulgur is tender and the stock has been absorbed. Check the seasoning.

Serve the pilaf spooned with yoghurt and sprinkled with the herbs and more chilli flakes.

Pastilla

Serve with harissa (page 199). This can also be made into individual parcels.

Serves 4

1 tablespoon olive oil
2 onions, roughly chopped
80g/generous ⅓ cup butter, melted
700g/1lb 9oz diced kid meat
3 garlic cloves, finely chopped
1 teaspoon ground cinnamon
2 teaspoons ras al hanout
pinch of saffron strands (optional)
200ml/scant 1 cup chicken or kid stock
   (or use water)
50g/1¾oz chopped almonds
   or pistachios

50g/1¾oz dried dates, apricots or raisins,
   roughly chopped
1 tablespoon honey
3 eggs, beaten
small bunch of parsley or coriander
   (cilantro), finely chopped
5 large sheets of filo (phyllo) pastry
1 tablespoon icing (confectioners') sugar
salt and freshly ground black pepper

Heat the olive oil in a pan, add the onions and fry for about 10 minutes, or until soft and beginning to brown. Add 1 tablespoon of the melted butter to the pan, turn up the heat, add the meat and cook for 10 minutes until any liquid released from the meat has evaporated and the meat is just beginning to colour. Add the garlic, half the cinnamon and all the remaining spices, and fry for 1 minute more.

Add the stock and season with salt and pepper to taste, then cover and simmer for about 45 minutes or until the meat is cooked and just tender. Remove the lid and increase the heat to reduce the liquid in the pan to about 150ml/⅔ cup, then add the nuts, dried fruit and honey. Add the eggs to the pan and gently cook until the mixture starts to resemble scrambled eggs, then add the herbs, remove from the heat and put to one side.

Preheat the oven to 180°C/350°F/gas mark 4.

Take a sheet of filo (phyllo) pastry and brush it with melted butter. Drape it over an oven dish large enough to fit all the meat mixture, gently pushing it into the corners, and leaving the edges overhanging the dish. Repeat with another sheet of filo, this time placing it at a right angle to the first. Repeat with the next 2 sheets of filo to form a large pastry case with no tears.

Spoon the meat mixture into a heap in the centre of the pastry, then fold the overhanging filo over the meat to make a pie. Lay the final filo sheet on top, brush with butter and tuck under any corners.

Bake in the oven for about 30 minutes until the pastry is crisp and golden brown. Remove from the oven and allow to cool a little before dusting it with the icing (confectioners') sugar and the rest of the cinnamon to serve.

Mongolian Crisp Fried Lettuce Rolls

This can also be cooked entirely on the hob, for about 1½ hours in total. The meal can be bulked up with the addition of cooked rice or noodles in the lettuce leaves, or on the side.

Serves 4

2 tablespoons honey or brown sugar
600g/1lb 5oz boneless kid shoulder, shank or breast, chopped into large chunks
2 tablespoons finely chopped fresh ginger
1 cinnamon or cassia stick
2 star anise
1 teaspoon fennel seeds
1 dried red chilli
3½ tablespoons dark soy sauce

150ml/⅔ cup rice wine
½–1 teaspoon ground Sichuan pepper or dried chilli flakes (optional)

to serve
crisp lettuce leaves
1 cucumber, peeled, deseeded and sliced
½ bunch of spring onions (scallions), finely sliced

Preheat the oven to 180°C/350°F/gas mark 4.

Put the honey in a large ovenproof pan that has a lid, or a flameproof casserole, heat until it begins to caramelise then stir in the meat, ginger and whole spices.

Add the soy and rice wine, then add about 200ml/scant ¼ cup water. Bring to the boil, cover tightly and bake in the oven for about 1 hour, or until tender.

Uncover and cook on the hob until the liquid has reduced by about half. Remove the meat and put it in the fridge to cool, then strain the sauce into a pan (discard the aromatics). Boil the liquid until

reduced to a sticky sauce; set aside and keep warm for serving. Once the meat has cooled, pull it into bite-sized pieces and dust with the Sichuan pepper or chilli, if using.

Fry the pulled pieces of meat in a dry frying pan over a high heat, or grill under a high heat, until the outside is really crispy and the middle is hot, checking the seasoning (remembering the sauce is quite highly seasoned).

To serve, fill the lettuce leaves with spoonfuls of the meat and sauce, top with the cucumber and spring onions (scallions), then roll them up to eat. Napkins are recommended!

James Lyon Shaw

Devonshire Kid Goat Hotpot

I'll leave you in the capable hands of James of The Jugged Hare:

'Half the battle of convincing people to eat goat was always changing the perception that it is tough old meat only fit for a curry. The best way we got people to try it was to use the goat meat in familiar and favourite recipes that would traditionally be done with lamb or even venison.

I developed this recipe for The Jugged Hare menu a few years ago and it was such a firm favourite it almost out sold out as a signature dish!

You can adapt this recipe to make it a bit simpler by removing the different cuts or the offal but I like the variety of textures and flavours it gives, and it brings the traditional Lancashire hotpot bang up to date while giving a nose-to-tail experience of goat all in one dish!

A bit of pre-planning is needed for the first part of this dish, so get ready in advance and plan the cooking times for each section of the recipe.'

Serves 4

½ shoulder of kid on the bone
rapeseed oil, for cooking
150g/5oz lean minced (ground) kid
200g/7oz kid neck fillet, trimmed and diced
4 kid kidneys, quartered, fat removed
200g/7oz kid liver, skinned and diced
1 white onion, diced
2 celery sticks, diced
1 large carrot, diced
bunch of baby turnips, halved
1 teaspoon tomato paste
20g/2⅓ tablespoons plain
    (all-purpose) flour
500ml/2 cups strong lamb stock
    (use 2 stock cubes, or goat stock if you
    have some)
150ml/⅔ cup red wine

4 sprigs of thyme
4 mint leaves, thinly sliced
2 bay leaves
500g/1lb 2oz large potatoes,
    peeled and sliced
100g/scant ½ cup butter, melted
1 x 4-bone rack of kid, French trimmed
salt and freshly ground black pepper

for roasting the shoulder

5 sprigs of thyme
5 sprigs of rosemary
5 garlic cloves, peeled and sliced
olive oil
mixture of roughly chopped root veg,
    such as onions, carrots, celery and
    turnips

Preheat the oven to 150°C/300°F/gas mark 2.

Season the shoulder well, then use a small, sharp knife to make slits all over. Stud with thyme, rosemary leaves, garlic slices and douse generously with oil. Season all over with salt and pepper.

Put the roughly chopped root veg in a roasting tray and place the shoulder on top. Cover securely in foil and slow-cook in the oven for 4 hours, until the meat falls off the bone at the touch of a fork. Depending on your oven and the size of the shoulder, this may take a bit longer. Once it's done, just flake the meat off the

bone into fork-sized pieces and set this aside. Increase the oven temperature to 160°C/325°F/gas mark 3.

Heat a little rapeseed oil in a large flameproof casserole, add the minced meat and brown off in batches until heavily caramelised and completely separated, almost to the point of being crispy. Remove from the pan and brown off the neck meat in the same way, then remove and repeat with the kidneys and liver, keeping all the cuts separate once coloured.

Fry the onion, celery, carrot and turnips in the casserole in a little oil until soft and golden. Add the tomato paste and sprinkle over the flour, then cook for a couple of minutes, stirring out any lumps.

Pour in the stock and red wine, add the thyme, mint and bay leaves, then bring to the boil. Stir in the neck meat and simmer for 30 minutes, then take off the heat. Fold in the mince, fried kidneys and liver, and the flaked shoulder meat.

Arrange the sliced potatoes on top of the meat, then drizzle with a little of the butter. Cover with a heavy lid and cook in the oven for about 1½ hours until the potatoes are cooked. Remove the lid, brush the potatoes with a little more butter, then turn the oven up to 180°C/350°F/gas mark 4 to brown the potatoes, or finish under the grill for 5–8 minutes until brown.

Meanwhile, heat a little oil in a heavy-based, ovenproof frying pan (or ideally a cast-iron skillet). Season the rack then seal in the hot pan until brown on all sides. Transfer to the hot oven for 6 minutes while the potatoes are browning, then take out to rest for 4 minutes.

Carve the rack into cutlets, exposing the beautiful pink meat, and lay neatly on top of the hotpot with the rack bones rising up and crossing slightly.

Serve at the table in the casserole dish. I like to serve this with buttered Savoy cabbage or braised red cabbage.

Darren Goodwin

Kid Goat Pressed Shoulder
and Potato Terrine

Darren was one of our first customers and knows our product as well as anyone. His cooking is characterized by his attention to detail and his total lack of ego. Darren just wants to cook nice food for people. This terrine is beautiful on its own with some pickles, but it's also an excellent side for a roasted saddle (page 165).

Serves 8 as a starter

2 tablespoons olive oil
½ shoulder of kid on the bone
1 onion, roughly chopped
2 carrots, roughly chopped
1 whole head of garlic, halved horizontally
2 celery sticks, roughly chopped

4 sprigs of rosemary, chopped
1 litre/4 cups chicken stock; plus more if needed
6–8 potatoes, peeled and very thinly sliced using a mandoline
salt and freshly ground black pepper

Preheat the oven to 180°C/350°F/gas mark 4.

In a flameproof casserole large enough for the shoulder to fit in, heat the oil and then brown the shoulder over a moderate heat. Add the vegetables, garlic and rosemary and, once all the vegetables are also coloured, add the stock. The meat must be covered with liquid, so add a little more stock or water as required.

Cover the dish with a lid or a good layer of foil and bake in the oven for 4 hours until completely tender. Remove from the oven and leave to cool slightly, then remove the meat from the stock and strain the stock through a fine sieve (reserving 400ml/generous 1½ cups). Pick through the meat, discarding any bone or large pieces of fat.

Increase the oven temperature to 190°C/375°F/gas mark 5.

Line a loaf tin or similar with baking parchment, leaving a good amount overhanging the edges so the parchment will completely wrap the potatoes.

Seasoning each layer with salt and a little pepper, add 2 layers of sliced potato to the base of the lined tin, then 1 layer of braised meat, 2 layers of potato, another layer of braised meat and finally 2 more layers of potato. Pour in the reserved stock until it almost covers the potato (push down on the potatoes to check). Fold over the parchment and wrap the loaf tin in foil.

Bake in the oven for 45 minutes or until a skewer or small knife will slide in and out of the terrine with ease. Allow to cool slightly, then add a tray to the top of the tin so that it fits inside, add a couple of food cans for weights and leave overnight in the fridge to compress and become firm. Bring to room temperature before slicing and serving.

Yotam Ottolenghi

Goat Shawarma with Yoghurt Flatbreads and Pickled Watermelon Rind

This is a dish developed for Yotam's 2016 debut at Meatopia, the fire and meat festival held at Tobacco Dock in London every September. It has since made its way on to his restaurant menus. I confess to being a little speechless when I saw the man himself serving up our goat that day. How far we had come from four goats in a field! It's a superb recipe. The flatbreads and pickled watermelon rind have a thousand uses beyond the shawarma too, so are worth mastering.

Serves 6–8

1 leg of kid on the bone, with fat, about 2.5–3kg/5½–6½lb
8 tablespoons goat's yoghurt, to drizzle on the meat before serving (optional)

for the shawarma marinade

2 teaspoons black peppercorns
5 whole cloves
½ teaspoon cardamom pods
¼ teaspoon fenugreek seeds
1 teaspoon fennel seeds
1 tablespoon cumin seeds
1 star anise
½ cinnamon stick
½ a nutmeg, grated
¼ teaspoon ground ginger
1 tablespoon sweet paprika
1 tablespoon sumac
¾ tablespoon Maldon sea salt
25g/1oz fresh ginger, grated

3 garlic cloves, crushed
40g/1½oz chopped coriander (cilantro), stems and leaves
60ml/¼ cup lemon juice
120g/½ cup groundnut oil

for the salad

1 medium kohlrabi (about 200g/7oz), peeled and julienned
10 spring onions (scallions), julienned
40g/1½oz coriander (cilantro) leaves with stems
40g/1½oz mint leaves, torn
500g/1lb 2oz watermelon cubes from the pickled rind (see 189)
300g/10½oz pickled watermelon rind (see 189)
160g/5½oz pomegranate seeds
60g/¼ cup olive oil
1 teaspoon Maldon sea salt

Put the first 8 spices for the marinade in a cast-iron pan and dry-roast over a medium-high heat for 1–2 minutes, until the spices begin to pop and release their aromas; take care not to burn them. Add the nutmeg, ground ginger and paprika, toss for a few more seconds, just to heat them, then transfer to a spice grinder. Blend the spices to a uniform powder then transfer to a medium bowl and stir in the remaining marinade ingredients.

Use a small, sharp knife to score the leg in a few places, making 1.5cm/²⁄₃in deep slits through the fat and meat to allow the marinade to seep in. Place in a large roasting tin and rub the marinade all over the meat, using your hands to massage the meat well. Cover the tin with foil and leave aside for at least a couple of hours or, preferably, chill in the fridge overnight.

Preheat the oven to 150°C/300°F/gas mark 2.

Remove the foil and put the leg in the oven with its fatty side facing up. Roast for about 4–5 hours, until the meat is completely tender, adding a cup of boiling water to the tin after 30 minutes of roasting and using this liquid to baste the meat every hour or so. Add more water, as needed, making sure there is always about 5mm/¼in in the bottom of the tin. For the last 3 hours, cover the leg with foil to prevent the spices from burning. Once done, remove from the oven and leave to rest for 10 minutes

Meanwhile, mix all the salad ingredients together in a bowl with 1 tablespoon of the watermelon rind pickling liquor. Stir gently and set aside.

Carve the leg and serve with the yoghurt flatbreads, pickled watermelon and salad, drizzled with goat's yoghurt.

Yoghurt Flatbreads

Makes 8

1 teaspoon fast-action dried yeast
180ml/¾ cup warm water
1 teaspoon caster sugar
120g/½ cup plain yoghurt

250g/generous 1¾ cups plain
   (all-purpose) flour, plus extra for dusting
250g/1¾ cups strong bread flour
1 teaspoon salt
100g/8 tablespoons ghee

Whisk the yeast, warm water and sugar together in a small bowl, set aside for 15 minutes until it starts to froth, then tip into an electric mixer with a dough hook attached. Add the yoghurt, flours and salt and knead slowly for 2 minutes, to combine; the dough will be quite dry. Turn up the speed to medium-high and knead for 5 minutes, until the dough is smooth yet firm. Roll into a sausage and cut into 8 pieces. Roll each piece into a ball, put on a large tray, cover with a clean tea towel (dish towel) and set aside to double in size, about 90 minutes.

Roll out each ball, one at a time, on a lightly floured surface into a circle 18–20cm/7–8in diameter and 1–2mm/¹⁄₁₆in thick.

Melt 1 tablespoon ghee in a non-stick frying pan over a medium-high heat and fry the bread for 3–4 minutes, turning halfway, until golden-brown on both sides. Set aside, cover with a clean tea towel and repeat with the remaining dough and ghee.

Pickled Watermelon Rind

1 small watermelon (about 1.5kg/3¼lb),
    seedless if possible
3 tablespoons salt
200ml/¾ cup cider vinegar
250ml/1 cup rice vinegar

60g/⅓ cup caster (superfine) sugar
½ teaspoon whole cloves
1 teaspoon yellow mustard seeds
1 cinnamon stick
1 teaspoon black peppercorns

Using a vegetable peeler, shave off the dark green outer skin from the watermelon and discard. You want to leave the firm white rind intact, so don't shave down too deeply. Use a large, sharp knife to cut the watermelon in half and then each half into 3 or 4 wedges. Next, slice between the white rind and the red flesh. Cut the flesh into 3cm/1¼in cubes and remove any seeds. Set aside the watermelon cubes for the salad mix. Cut the white rind into long thin strips – about 4–5cm/1½ –2in long and about 3mm/¹/₁₀in thick – and set aside in a large bowl.

Pour 1 litre/4 cups water into a medium saucepan and add the salt. Bring to the boil, stir to dissolve the salt, then remove from the heat. Set aside to cool then pour it over the watermelon rind. Store in the fridge, covered, for 24 hours, then drain the rind, rinse it under fresh water and set aside.

Place the cider vinegar, rice vinegar, sugar and spices in a small saucepan with 200ml/¾ cup of water. Bring to the boil, then simmer over a medium heat for 2 minutes to dissolve the sugar. Set aside to cool and then pour over the rind. Set aside until ready to use. It will be ready to eat after just 1 hour but you can leave it at this stage, in a sterilized jar, for months: the longer the rind gets pickled, the softer it will be and the more intense it will taste.

Jeremy Lee

Kid Pie

Cabrito's first sale was to Jeremy Lee at Quo Vadis on 27 March 2012 and we've been on and off the menu ever since. Few chefs so effortlessly make beautiful, wholesome and comforting food. If I could choose someone to cook my last meal on earth, I would choose Jeremy – and I might well ask for this pie.

Serves 6–8

1kg/2lb 3oz boneless kid shoulder, chopped into good thumb-sized pieces
1kg/2lb 3oz boneless kid leg, chopped into good thumb-sized pieces
handful of any heart, liver, kidneys or well-cleaned pluck, chopped small
2 tablespoons sunflower oil
20g/2⅓ tablespoons plain (all-purpose) flour
250g/9oz unsmoked pancetta, finely chopped
1 large onion, chopped into large pieces
3 garlic cloves, peeled but left whole
4 celery sticks, chopped into large pieces
3 large carrots, chopped into large pieces
500ml/2 cups dry white wine
small sprig each of rosemary, thyme, sage and bay leaves, tied in a bundle
500ml/2 cups good chicken stock
salt and freshly ground black pepper

for the pastry

250g/9oz suet
500g/3¾ cups self-raising (self-rising) flour
1 egg, plus 1 extra beaten egg, to glaze
1–2 tablespoons milk

Season all the kid meat and offal. In one large or two small frying pans, heat the oil over a medium heat and add the seasoned meat and offal in batches. As the meat is browning, dust it lightly with flour, and remove once it is all browned beautifully.

Add the pancetta, onion, garlic, celery and carrots to the pan/s and cook, covered, in the residual oil until soft and starting to colour. (Should there be any bones from the kid, you might pop these in the oven, roast until golden brown and add these into the next step.)

Transfer the vegetables and meat to a braising pan with the wine, herb bundle and stock. Simmer for 2 hours over a very gentle heat, taking care that the stock doesn't reduce too much. If it's too liquid-y, simmer for longer.

Preheat the oven to 200°C/400°F/gas mark 6. Check the stew seasoning and remove the herb bundle, then transfer to a pie dish.

For the pastry, rub the suet into the flour with a good pinch of salt until you have a nice crumb. Separately, mix the egg and milk in a bowl and then mix into the flour until you have a big clump. Do not over-mix. Roll out the pastry straight away – there is no need to rest – and lay it atop the pie. Trim the edges as required.

Brush the pastry with the beaten egg and bake for 35–40 minutes. Keep a beady eye on any overenthusiastic colouring of the pastry, in which case you might need to put a little foil over the top.

I would serve this with some lovely mashed potatoes and buttered cabbage.

Basics

Baharat Spice Blend

You can up the quantities here to make more – just keep the same proportions.

2 teaspoons cracked black pepper
2 teaspoons ground cumin
1 teaspoon ground coriander
1 teaspoon ground nutmeg

1 teaspoon ground green cardamon
1 teaspoon ground cinnamon
½ teaspoons ground cloves

Combine all the ingredients together until well mixed. Store in an airtight jar and keep away from direct sunlight.

Salsa Verde

This can also be made in a food processor, though try not to over-blend it. Tarragon and chervil can be an interesting replacement for the basil and mint. Chopped gherkins or cornichons can be added too.

Makes about 250ml/1 cup

4 anchovy fillets, rinsed if packed in salt
2 garlic cloves, finely chopped
large bunch of flatleaf parsley,
    leaves picked
small bunch of basil or mint
    (or a combination), leaves picked
2 tablespoons salted capers, rinsed

and roughly chopped
1 tablespoon Dijon mustard
2 tablespoons red wine vinegar
    or lemon juice, or to taste
about 100ml/scant ½ cup good quality
    extra virgin olive oil
salt and freshly ground black pepper

Mash the anchovies and garlic together in mortar and pestle, then gradually add the herbs and capers and pound to a rough paste. (Or chop the herbs, anchovies, capers and garlic together on a big board, using a large knife.)

Stir in the mustard and vinegar or lemon juice, then slowly whisk in the olive oil until you achieve your desired consistency. Taste and add more vinegar or lemon juice if you like, plus salt and pepper to taste.

This is best eaten the day it is made, but you can store it in a jar with a thin layer of oil on the top in the fridge, for up to 3 days.

Mustard BBQ Sauce

This sauce from South Carolina is traditionally made with yellow mustard, but you can also try it with Dijon. Make it the day before to allow the flavours to develop.

Makes about 400ml/1¾ cups

3 tablespoons butter
200g/7oz Dijon or yellow mustard
100g/½ cup brown sugar
50ml/3½ tablespoons cider vinegar
2 tablespoons tomato ketchup

1 tablespoon Worcestershire sauce
1 teaspoon hot sauce (page 198) or chipotle sauce (page 200), or more to taste
1 teaspoon freshly ground black pepper

Melt the butter in a pan over a gentle heat, add the remaining ingredients, mix well until well combined and the sugar has dissolved, then remove from the heat and leave to cool.

This will keep, refrigerated, for at least a week.

Zhug

You can use a food processor to make this, but using ground spices instead of whole.

Makes about 250ml/1 cup

seeds of 4 green cardamom pods
1 teaspoon coriander seeds
½ teaspoon cumin seeds
6 garlic cloves, chopped
4–8 fresh green chillies, stems removed and deseeded (depending on your taste and the heat of the chillies)

small bunch of coriander (cilantro), roughly chopped
small bunch of flatleaf parsley, roughly chopped (or just use a big bunch of coriander)
4 tablespoons olive oil
salt and freshly ground black pepper

Crush all the seeds in a mortar and pestle with a pinch of salt, then add the garlic and chillies and grind to a very coarse paste before adding the herbs and grinding to a coarse paste. Add the oil gradually, then season to taste.

This is best eaten the day it is made, but you can store it in a jar in the fridge for up to 3 days, with a thin layer of oil on the top.

Chimichurri

Use as a sauce for BBQ kid, or as a marinade. I like the loose texture, but it can be pulsed to a coarse purée in a blender or using a mortar and pestle.

Makes about 250ml/1 cup

4 tablespoons red wine vinegar
½ teaspoon salt
2 garlic cloves, finely chopped
1 small shallot, finely chopped
  (or use ½ bunch trimmed spring
  onions/scallions)
½ teaspoon dried chilli flakes,
  or more to taste

1 teaspoon dried oregano
small bunch of parsley, leaves finely
  chopped
2 tablespoons fresh oregano, chopped
  (optional)
6 tablespoons extra virgin olive oil
  (or vegetable oil)
freshly ground black pepper

Mix the vinegar, salt, garlic and shallot in a bowl and put to one side for 10 minutes. Stir in the rest of the ingredients, with pepper to taste, and allow to flavours to develop for an hour or so before serving.

Hot Sauce

Try roasting the chillies in a hot oven until charred, before chopping, for a variation.

Be careful when handling Scotch bonnets – ideally wear latex gloves when chopping them, be very careful to not scratch your eyes (or anything else!), and wash your hands thoroughly after.

This sauce can start to ferment, so if keeping for a while store it in the fridge in a sterilized bottle.

Makes about 150ml/⅓ cup

5–10 Scotch bonnets
  (or use another fresh chilli)
3½ tablespoons wine vinegar
  or cider vinegar

½ teaspoon salt
1–2 teaspoons sugar

Roughly chop the Scotch bonnets (see recipe introduction), removing the stalks and any excess seed membrane. Put them into a small food processor or blender with the vinegar and salt, and blend until smooth. Pour into a pan and bring to the boil. Turn down the heat and simmer for 5 minutes until cooked.

Add 50ml/3¼ tablespoons water and the sugar, to taste, then stir and simmer for a further few minutes until thickened to your liking. Remove from the heat and allow to cool, then blend again until completely smooth. Store in a jar or bottle in the fridge.

Chilli and Garlic Chutney

You can use fresh chillies for this too.

Makes about 150ml/²⁄₃ cup

8–10 dried red chillies
8 garlic cloves, peeled but left whole
1 tablespoon chopped fresh ginger
1 tablespoon lemon juice or vinegar

½ teaspoon salt
1 teaspoon ground coriander
1 teaspoon ground cumin
3 tablespoons vegetable oil

Soak the chillies in boiling water for 15 minutes, then drain. Put into a food processor with the remaining ingredients except the oil, and blend to a very coarse paste. Fry the paste in the oil for 5 minutes until thick and aromatic.

This will keep for at least a week, stored in a jar or bottle in the fridge.

Harissa

Makes about 250ml/1 cup

100g/3½oz fresh red chillies,
   halved lengthways and deseeded
1 red (bell) pepper, deseeded
   and cut into quarters
2 tomatoes, halved
1 teaspoon ground cumin, toasted

1 teaspoon ground caraway, toasted
1 teaspoon ground coriander, toasted
2 garlic cloves
2 teaspoons red wine vinegar
2 tablespoons extra virgin olive oil
salt

Put the chillies, (bell) pepper and tomatoes, skin side down, in a frying pan and dry-fry for about 10 minutes, until scorched and slightly softened.

Transfer to a blender or food processor with the remaining ingredients, adding salt to taste, and blend until smooth. Check the seasoning.

Store in the fridge with a thin layer of olive oil on top to seal. It will keep for at least week.

Aïoli

Makes about 250ml/1 cup
2 egg yolks
5 garlic cloves, crushed to a paste
1 teaspoon Dijon mustard

about 200ml/scant 1 cup olive oil
lemon juice, to taste (a good squeeze
    at least)
salt and freshly ground black pepper

Place the egg yolks, garlic, mustard and a big pinch of salt in a small bowl and beat together using a balloon whisk.

A couple of drops at a time, add 1 tablespoon of the oil, whisking quickly to get the emulsion going. Slowly add the rest of the olive oil in a slow stream, whisking all the time, until fully emulsified. You can add a couple of tablespoons of water if you want a looser consistency.

Add lemon juice and pepper to taste and store in the fridge, for up to 2 days.

Chipotle Sauce

Makes about 350ml/1½ cups
40g/1½oz whole dried chipotle chillies
6 garlic cloves, peeled but left whole
3½ tablespoons vegetable
    or olive oil
salt

Fry the chipotle chillies and garlic in half the oil, stirring, for about 5 minutes (the chillies will be puffed and the garlic browned).

Set the garlic aside and transfer the chipotles to a bowl. Cover with hot water and leave to soak for about 15 minutes, until soft. Drain and remove the stems, seeds and veins, then purée in a food processor or blender with the garlic and about 200ml/scant 1 cup water.

Heat the rest of the oil in the same pan over a medium-high heat. When hot, add the puréed salsa and cook, stirring occasionally, until thickened, about 10 minutes. Season to taste with salt.

Yoghurt Sauce

You can add 3½ tablespoons tahini mixed with 3½ tablespoons water to this – a blender being the most effective method.

200ml/scant 1 cup plain yoghurt
juice of ½ lemon
½ garlic clove, crushed
salt and freshly ground black pepper

Mix together the yoghurt, lemon juice and garlic, and add salt and pepper to taste.

Chopped Salad

Best if everything is chopped roughly to the same size, adding or removing ingredients as you wish. Mix and match the herbs too, and add green olives and/or feta, if you like.

Serves 4–6

6 tbsp olive oil
juice from ½ lemon
1 tsp dried oregano or mint
1 small garlic clove, crushed
1 gem lettuce, finely chopped
1 red pepper, finely chopped
1 bunch spring onions (scallions) or
   a small red onion, finely chopped

1 cucumber, peeled, deseeded and finely
   chopped
3 ripe tomatoes, finely chopped
1 bunch mint, coriander (cilantro)
   or flatleaf parsley, roughly chopped
salt and freshly ground black pepper

Whisk together the oil, lemon juice, oregano or mint, and garlic in small bowl. Season to taste with salt and pepper.

Combine all the remaining salad ingredients in a large bowl. Pour over the dressing and toss to coat. Taste to check the seasoning.

Acknowledgements

Jeez, where to start...?

Sarah Lavelle, thanks for believing a goat book would work and giving me the freedom to write the book I have.

Thank you to the team at Quadrille and designer Will Webb for producing a beautiful book. I still can't quite believe it. And at Farm Africa, Charlotte Senior has been a constant source of enthusiasm and support.

For the research that went into the book, there is a long list of thanks:

Margit Groenevelt DVM Dip. ECSRHM, thank you for guiding me though the rumen and patiently explaining complex animal health and welfare issues to a layman.

To Phil Ormerod, for explaining the practical alongside the theory, and helping me to understand modern farming.

James Mwololo of Farm Africa, over a few terrible Skype lines to Kenya, gave me a wonderful insight into the fantastic work the charity does. This is the reality of the foreign aid budget, folks – money well spent.

Thank you to Harry West, professor of Anthropology at Exeter University who pointed me in the right direction when I started looking back into early farming. And thank you to Filipe Pereira and Antonio Amorim from the University of Porto, on whose research projects I have drawn for much of the historical information.

Thank you to Ivan Day for a magical five-hour history lesson in his Cambrian farmhouse, which gave me the confidence to tell the tale of Man and Goat. It wouldn't have happened without you.

Thank you to all the chefs that have given recipes for the book. I am so grateful that you've helped to light up the pages.

Thanks to Mike Lusmore and Stephanie Boote.

To Matt Williamson, you are brilliant. You make it all look so easy.

Tiffany Jesse and John Robertson. Without you two there would never have been any goats. We owe so much to you and to Little Winters.

To Will and Caroline Atkinson, thank you for everything – the advice, the support, the encouragement, the cheese, and for being Cabrito's conscience.

On a more personal note:

To Mickell, Dadine and Danny Doe. Grandparents *extraordinaires*. Your support and amazing emergency-skills childcare have made this book possible.

Finally, to Moles, who does all the hard work, like raising our children and earning the money while I swan around trying to flog stuff. This book is for you. Everything is.

General Index

kid rendang 60
rogan josh 46
West African peanut curry 58

D

dairy goats 20–7
devilled kidneys 114
Devonshire kid goat hotpot 181–3
Domesday Book 19
domestication of goats 14–15
dukka 108
dumplings: goat dumplings 104
   goat ragù wonton, XO and burnt cabbage 116–19
   steamed dumplings filled with goat meat 110

E

Eagle-style seared kid sandwich 86
eggs: matambre 156
Ethiopia 34–7

F

Farm Africa 34–7
farming methods 20–7
fatayer 172
fermenting milk 15–16
flatbreads, yoghurt 188
frying kid chops 102

G

garlic: aïoli 200
   chilli and garlic chutney 199
   chipotle sauce 200
   kid with almonds 61
genomics 22
A German Brewet 68
goulash, heart 66
Greek sausage, orange and leek loukaniko Greek
   sausage 82
gremolata 52
grilling kid chops 102

H

haricot beans: kid cassoulet 174
harissa 199
hay barbecue goat 132
heart goulash 66
herb-crusted rack of kid 162–4
history 14–20
honey: goat kebabs with peaches, honey, almonds
   and mint 136
hot sauce 198
hotpot, Devonshire kid goat 181–3
humita 64
hummus: herb-crusted rack of kid with hummus
   162–4
   twice-cooked kid with hummus 158

J

jerk marinade 125

K

kebabs: goat kebabs with peaches, honey, almonds
   and mint 136
   marinades for 122–6
keema: goat keema 71
   quick keema naan 48
kibbeh 98
kibbeh nayeh 101
kidneys: devilled kidneys 114
   Devonshire kid goat hotpot 181–3
kleftiko 160
kofta 97
kohlrabi: salad 187
korma, kid 44

L

labneh: kid, lentil and labneh salad 108
lactose intolerance 15–16
lahmacun 171
leather 32–4
leeks: orange and leek loukaniko Greek sausage 82
leftover kid, anchovy, bitter leaf and celery salad 161
lemon: butterflied leg of kid with preserved lemon
   127
lentils: goat dumplings 104
   kid, lentil and labneh salad 108
lettuce rolls, Mongolian crisp fried 180
liver: Devonshire kid goat hotpot 181–3
   liver with cumin and chilli 94

M

marinades 122–6
   jerk 125
   Mexican chilli citrus 126
   pinchos morunos 122
   Sichuan 122
   souvlaki 125
matambre 156
mayonnaise: aïoli 200
meatballs 96–7
   kibbeh 98
   kibbeh nayeh 101
   kofta 97
   sheftalia 100
merguez 81
methane 22–3
Mexican chilli citrus marinade 126
milk 20, 23
   aromatic kid with aubergine 45
   fermenting 15–16
Millington, Jack 32–4
mole, kid 50
Mongolian crisp fried lettuce rolls 180
moussaka, kid 173
mushrooms: herb-crusted rack of kid 162–4
mustard BBQ sauce 197

N

naan, quick keema 48

O

onions: burgers with halloumi, red onion salad and tzatziki 138
  crying leg boulangère 154
  kid biryani 170
  kid cassoulet 174
  smoked shoulder of kid goat with berbere 140–3
oranges: Mexican chilli citrus marinade 126
  orange and leek loukaniko Greek sausage 82
osso buco, kid 52
Ötzi the Iceman 12–14, 32–3

P

pancetta: kid pie 190
panko breadcrumbs: schnitzel 88
paprika: heart goulash 66
parsley: chimichurri 198
  salsa verde 196
pasta sauces 84
pastilla 178
pastries: fatayer 172
  lahmacun 171
  pastilla 178
pastry 190
peaches: goat kebabs with peaches, honey, almonds and mint 136
peanuts: suya kid chops 128
  West African peanut curry 58
peas: goat keema 71
peppers: aromatic kid with aubergine 45
  Cabrito al Disco 64
  harissa 199
  heart goulash 66
  humita 64
  kid cutlets with a chickpea, pepper and tomato casserole 112
  lahmacun 171
  leg wrapped in vine leaves 148
  matambre 156
  zab 152
Persian kofta 97
pickled watermelon rind 189
pies: kid pie 190
  see also pastries
pilaf: kid, cabbage, bulgur wheat and tomato pilaf 176
pinchos morunos marinade 122
pine nuts: kibbeh 98
  Persian kofta 97
  twice-cooked kid with hummus 158
pistachios: kid shank, apricot and pistachio tagine 54
pomegranate seeds: salad 187
pork: goat dumplings 104
potatoes: crying leg boulangère 154
  curry goat 62
  Devonshire kid goat hotpot 181–3
  kid goat pressed shoulder and potato terrine 184
  kleftiko 160
prosciutto: saltimbocca 92

puntarelle: leftover kid, anchovy, bitter leaf and celery salad 161

R

ragù (from leftovers) 93
raisins: twice-cooked kid with hummus 158
rendang, kid 60
restaurants 29–32
rhubarb, kid khoresht with 56
rice: boned shoulder stuffed with spiced rice 146
  kid biryani 170
roasts: boned shoulder stuffed with spiced rice 146
  crying leg boulangère 154
  herb-crusted rack of kid 162–4
  kid saddle with black pudding, clams and a wild garlic crumb 165–6
  kleftiko 160
  leg wrapped in vine leaves 148
  matambre 156
  slow-roast baharat shoulder 151
  twice-cooked kid with hummus 158
  zab 152
rogan josh 46

S

sage: saltimbocca 92
salads 187
  kid, lentil and labneh salad 108
  leftover kid, anchovy, bitter leaf and celery salad 161
  chopped 201
salsa verde 196
saltimbocca 92
sandwiches: 'Bife Ana' 86
sauces: aïoli 200
  broccoli and rosemary pasta sauce 84
  chimichurri 198
  chipotle sauce 200
  harissa 199
  hot sauce 198
  mustard BBQ sauce 197
  ragù (from leftovers) 93
  tomato, chilli and nutmeg pasta sauce 84
  yoghurt sauce 201
  zhug 197
sausages 80
  broccoli and rosemary pasta sauce 84
  kid cassoulet 174
  merguez 81
  orange and leek loukaniko Greek sausage 82
  tomato, chilli and nutmeg pasta sauce 84
schnitzel 88
scottadito, buttered 90
seeds: loin of goat, cracked wheat and anchovy dressing 106
shallots: goat dumplings 104
shawarma, goat 187
sheftalia 100
Sichuan marinade 122

Recipe index

Recipes suitable for goat or kid:

Recipes suitable for kid only: